IS INEQUALITY BAD
FOR OUR HEALTH?

"New Democracy Forum operates at a level of literacy and responsibility which is all too rare in our time." —John Kenneth Galbraith

Other books in the NEW DEMOCRACY FORUM series:

IS INEQUALITY BAD
FOR OUR HEALTH?

NORMAN DANIELS,
BRUCE KENNEDY, AND
ICHIRO KAWACHI

FOREWORD BY AMARTYA SEN

EDITED BY JOSHUA COHEN AND JOEL ROGERS
FOR *BOSTON REVIEW*

BEACON PRESS
BOSTON

BEACON PRESS
25 Beacon Street
Boston, Massachusetts 02108-2892
www.beacon.org

Beacon Press books
are published under the auspices of
the Unitarian Universalist Association of Congregations.

Printed in the United States of America

05 04 03 02 01 00   8 7 6 5 4 3 2 1

This book is printed on acid-free paper that meets the uncoated paper
ANSI/NISO specifications for permanence as revised in 1992.

Composition by Wilsted & Taylor Publishing Services

Library of Congress Cataloging-in-Publication Data
    Is inequality bad for our health? / [compiled by] Norman Daniels, Bruce
    Kennedy, and Ichiro Kawachi ; foreword by Amartya Sen ; edited by Joshua
    Cohen and Joel Rogers for Boston Review.
        p.   cm.
    ISBN 0-8070-0447-2 (pa)
        1. Medical care—Social aspects—United States.   2. Medical policy—
    Social aspects—United States.   3. Health services accessibility—United
    States.   4. Social medicine—United States.   5. Equality—Health
    aspects—United States.   I. Daniels, Norman, 1942–   II. Kennedy, Bruce,
    1950–   III. Kawachi, Ichiro.
    RA395.A3 I8   2000
    362.1'042'0973—dc21   00-039769

CONTENTS

3

FOREWORD

AMARTYA SEN

Dr. Samuel Johnson has argued, disputing the claims of equality, that "it is better that some should be unhappy than that none should be happy, which would be the case in a general state of equality."[1] The remark, as it stands, is slightly puzzling, since it is not at all clear why equality must necessarily take the form of everyone being unhappy, rather than everyone being happy. But the remark is also open to another interpretation. Dr. Johnson's point could have been that even though everyone being unhappy would be a state of equality, it would be wrong to celebrate that achievement on that ground, compared with an unequal state where many people are happy though not everyone is (despite the inequality involved). So equality cannot be an adequate basis of judgment, nor a sufficient guide to policy.

The point, seen in this way, seems fair enough. It would indeed be hard to sing the praise of equality if that meant equal misery for all. However, Dr. Johnson's observation, even when it is interpreted in this more plausible form, raises two other questions.

The first question is empirical. Can equality be achieved only by making everyone miserable and deprived? Or, more relevantly for practical policy, can inequality be *reduced* only by making everyone *more* miserable and deprived? Extending that inquiry, we can also ask: how pervasive is the alleged conflict between *distributive* and *aggregative* concerns? Insofar as Dr. Johnson's criticism is meant to be a general indictment of equality (rather than a particular judgment in a specific—and highly specified—case), much would depend on whether the reduction of inequality tends, in general, to make it harder to maintain and enhance efficiency, in the form of aggregative achievements. Dr. Johnson himself was inclined, it would appear, to believe in this kind of a conflict. For example, he responded to Boswell's frustration that "there was no civilized country in the world, where the misery of want in the lowest classes of the people was prevented," by prefacing his remark, quoted earlier, by the observation: "I believe, Sir, there is not."[2] There is an important issue to discuss here about the nature of the world in which we live, about how deep the tensions really are between aggregative and distributive concerns.[3]

The second issue is evaluational rather than empirical. Dr. Johnson talked about equality of happiness. Is happiness the best focus of attention in discussing equality? Or should it be income, wealth, opportunities, freedoms, or something else? The demands of equality in one "space" need not coincide with—and may even contradict—the requirements of equality in another space. In talking about needs of equality and their implications, we have to be clear what kind of equality should be the focus of our attention.[4] Both issues—aggregative/distributive and the choice of focus—are quite central to the analysis of equality.

HEALTH EQUITY AND SOCIOECONOMIC INEQUALITIES

The essays in this book make a significant contribution to both these issues. It is, in a broad sense, concerned with equity of health and health care. There is no suggestion that this is the only possible focus for analyzing equality, but plenty of reasoning which indicates, directly or indirectly, that this is an important ethical and political issue. The chosen point of departure of the book is the nature and determinants of health equity. In this sense, the collection of essays here is geared to investigating the implications of a particular answer to the "focal choice" question.

However, the empirical investigation of these implications takes us immediately from one focal space to another. In the principal paper of the volume, Norman Daniels, Bruce Kennedy, and Ichiro Kawachi criticize the tendency of "academic bioethics and popular discussion of health care reform" to concentrate too narrowly on "medicine at the point of delivery," as a result of which they have "inadequately attended to determinants of health 'upstream' from the medical system itself" (pp. 32–33). In contrast, they argue, with much evidence, that the social and economic determinants of health are very powerful, and "to act justly in health policy, we must have knowledge about the causal pathways through which socioeconomic (and other) inequalities work to produce differential health outcomes" (p. 19).

Thus the focus on health equality leads, through causal connections, to a concern for social and economic equalities. In the context of investigating health equity, the interest in the social and economic spaces is derivative, but given the strength of the relations, as Daniels, Kennedy, and Kawachi see them, the need for reducing social and economic inequalities emerges very powerfully for health reasons as well, in addition to its other merits. Also, on this analysis, the tension between choosing one focal space or another tends to be reduced to the extent that equality in one space seems to help promote equality in another.

In fact, Daniels, Kennedy, and Kawachi provide interesting analyses in linking their empirical conclusions to the influential reasoning on justice and equity presented by John Rawls, whose claim to being the preeminent moral philosopher of our times would be difficult (I believe, almost impossible) to dispute.[5] Daniels, Kennedy, and Kawachi point out that Rawlsian analysis leads to the conclusion that "a social contract designed to be fair to free and equal people would lead to equal basic liberties and equal opportunity and would permit inequalities only when they work to make the worst-off groups fare as well as possible" (p. 17). By combining this view of social justice with the empirical connections between socioeconomic inequalities and health equity, the principal authors identify a "striking result": to wit, "social justice is good for our health" (p. 33).

There is indeed a striking connection here. But we need to be careful in stating its precise content and implications. To that critical issue, I shall soon return, but first I want to comment on the "aggregative-distributive tension."

Distributive Achievements and Aggregative Goals

The empirical relationship between social and economic inequalities, on the one hand, and inequalities in the achievement of health, on the other, has received much attention in recent years. As it happens, some of the leading researchers in this field are among the contributors in this volume. As the propositions advanced by Daniels et al. get examined, the nuances of the identified connections receive pointed attention. One aspect of the findings that is particularly relevant is, as Sir Michael Marmot puts it, "where health inequalities are greatest, overall health status of the population is lower." Indeed, it is "difficult to lower the coronary heart disease mortality of the population if only part of the population is experiencing improvement" (Marmot, "Do Inequalities Matter?," p. 38).

This class of findings bears directly on the aggregative-distributive tension. Aggregate health is often best advanced by concentrating on the poorest, since this is where there is most scope for gaining further ground; but that very policy will have the effect of reducing distributive inequality as well. Thus the alleged tension between the two objectives may be far weaker than is often presumed. When we add to this the further fact that some ailments are linked through infectious spread (from cholera to AIDs), or through shared behavioral modes where one person's conduct influences another's (from smoking to high-fat food habits), it is easy to see that the complementarity between distributive and aggregative concerns can be even stronger. The attention that is frequently heaped on the allegedly pervasive implications of the distributive-aggregative tension may not always be justified.

Health Equity and Overall Justice

Even though most of the commentators are broadly in agreement with the empirical basis of the arguments presented by Daniels et al., the commentators have presented some interesting questions about the main conclusions of the principal authors, who in turn have provided a spirited response. The disputations are clear and engaging, and I leave the reader to judge what they make of these critical—and invariably interesting—arguments.

However, I should briefly return to the "focal choice" issue. It is possible to argue that the principal authors may be a little too readily inclined to conclude that all roads lead to Rome, which in this case is John Rawls's theory of justice.

Michael Marmot ("Do Inequalities Matter?") as well as Sudhir Anand and Fabienne Peter ("Equal Opportunity") have commented on some distinctions that the principal authors seem to overlook or underplay, and to those observations, the principal authors have given their reply. While readers will have to judge for themselves whether they are more convinced by the questions raised or by the answers given, I may take the liberty of commenting on some distinctions that, I would argue, should not be lost, or even distanced.

First, John Rawls's focus in his distributive maxim (the Difference Principle) is primarily on the distribution of resources (or "primary goods," as he calls them, such as income or health care), rather than the consequent achievements or the resulting freedoms of the individuals involved (such as good health or the capability to achieve good health). There is a significant distinction here that does not vanish merely because income, health care, and other resources tend to enhance health. Indeed, it is precisely because of these general connections between resource and achievements that resources are regarded as valuable at all. However, other factors, such as individual characteristics, climatic surroundings, regional epidemiology, etc., also influence health achievements. The fact that many of these influences cannot be picked up in some types of statistical analyses involving grouped data (particularly when the grouping is not linked to categories of epidemiological significance) is neither here nor there. But it could not be assumed that the elementary linkage between socioeconomic inequality and health achievement entails that there are no other influences on the achievement of health. An adequate policy approach to health has to take note not only of the influences on which this book concentrates, but also of a variety of other parameters, such as individually inherited proneness to disease, individual characteristics of disability, epidemiological hazards of particular regions, the influence of climatic variations, and so on.

Generally speaking, in making health policy, there is a need to distinguish resource-orientation from result-orientation, and in particular between equality in health achievements (or corresponding freedoms) and equality in the distribution of what can be generally called health resources.[6] Daniels's own attempt to include something of the former within the domain of "equality of opportunity" has many commendable features.[7] But it does not eliminate the fact that the two perspectives of "resource-orientation" and "result-orientation" can sharply differ. This empirical recognition is completely independent of which perspective—whether Rawlsian or not—that we use to interpret any particular dictum of the theory of justice.

Second, some difference is made also by how exactly inequality is seen. In the Rawlsian approach, the focus is entirely on the worst-off individuals. In comparing two groups, only if the worst-off individuals in the two groups happen to be equally badly off are we allowed to look at the distributional characteristics of others in the respective groups. But as the famous Black Report in Britain had brought out, and indeed as Daniels, Kennedy, and Kawachi summarize it, "differences in health outcome are not confined to the extremes of rich and poor but are observed across all levels of socioeconomic status" (p. 11).[8] Concentrating merely on the worst-off individuals (or groups of individuals) gives us, therefore, a less sensitive measure of inequality than we need for relating socioeconomic inequality to health inequality.

Third, the different components of socioeconomic affluence do not always move together. As Michael Marmot's work has shown, and as is rightly quoted by Daniels, Kennedy, and Kawachi, "steep gradients have been observed even among groups of individuals, such as British civil servants, who all have adequate access to health care, housing, and transport" (p. 11).[9] It is, of course, possible to aggregate the socioeconomic advantages exclusively in terms of their health effects (as if social and economic inequality matters only for their induced effects on health), but since these advantages also differentiate our lives in other ways as well, the health-effect-based aggregation need not coincide with other ways of taking note of economic affluence or social advantage. In this sense, the conclusion of the principal authors that "health is the by-product of justice" (p. 32) oversimplifies the demands of health equity vis-à-vis the extensive requirements of social justice. There are choices that remain, and they demand recognition.

Finally, even though the principal authors are right to

stress the need to avoid overconcentration on "medicine at the point of delivery" (paying inadequate attention to the "determinants of health 'upstream' from the medical system itself"), there are policy decisions to be made on the relative emphases to be placed on the two different kinds of determinants of health. Some countries or regions—from Costa Rica to Kerala in India—have achieved spectacular results in health improvement by enhancing health delivery (despite low income levels), and this issue remains alive today in the world, not least in the United States, where the entitlement to health delivery is still very unequally organized. This has some connection, along with other factors, with the remarkable fact that the people of Kerala, who are extremely poor in comparison with many American groups (including African-Americans), still live longer than these more economically affluent groups do. In emphasizing an underemphasized route to good health, we should not undermine other routes that also need attention.

A CONCLUDING REMARK

The point of making these distinctions is not, in any way, to reduce the importance of the empirical connections on which Daniels, Kennedy, and Kawachi base their analysis, nor to slight the important point that many of the tensions that are discussed abstractly in political philosophy or in policy making are substantially reduced in reality by the presence of these positive relations. Both the focal choice question and the distributive-aggregative tension are made less divisive as a result of these findings, on some of which I have commented. This is a more modest recognition than some claims that the principal authors have advanced, but it is nevertheless an extremely important part of an adequate understanding of the demands of health policy.

Many further distinctions remain, and the conflicting demands on policy making are not eliminated by the connections identified. But the principal authors are entirely right to argue that the conflicts may be far less severe than is frequently presumed. The complementarity between health equity and other kinds of justice is also a striking recognition. There is no real congruence here, but complementarity is itself an important connection.

In this timely and important book, the principal authors and the commentators have significantly enriched our understanding of the complementarities involved and their extensive implications for policy as well as theory. We have much reason to be grateful.

EDITORS' PREFACE

JOSHUA COHEN AND JOEL ROGERS

Reforming America's exclusionary health care system was one of Bill Clinton's first priorities as president. Clinton's plan collapsed, and eight years later more than 40 million Americans are still uninsured. But if this New Democracy Forum's lead article by Norman Daniels, Bruce Kennedy, and Ichiro Kawachi is right, something worse than the defeat of health care reform happened to public health over the past decade.

Drawing on a wide range of epidemiological studies, Daniels, Kennedy, and Kawachi argue that socioeconomic inequality itself is bad for our health: it is healthier to have higher income and live in a wealthier country, but also *to live in a more equal society.* So inequality—which has grown substantially since the 1970s—is arguably the dominant public health problem. From this striking assertion it follows that we need to broaden the terms of the health care debate, to shift away from an exclusive focus on expanding access to care (as important as that is) and toward redressing underlying socioeconomic inequality—through early childhood intervention, improved nutrition, better working conditions, and income redistribution.

The respondents to Daniels, Kennedy, and Kawachi dispute their analytical claims and political conclusions. Analytically, respondents ask how exactly inequality—as distinct from concentrations of poverty—produces bad health. And they also question the importance of inequality, as opposed to access to care, in explaining public health. On the practical side, several argue that changing the distribution of income may be far less feasible than improving access (especially to primary care). So even if economic justice might deliver greater gains, we are more likely to get improvements by concentrating on better access. These critics suggest that Daniels, Kennedy, and Kawachi are making the best the enemy of the good.

This disagreement is important. More important, though, is a point of agreement: that great social inequalities are unhealthy. And yet, for all the present talk of "health care reform" and the importance of the issue for Americans, this basic point is virtually absent from public debate.

1

JUSTICE IS GOOD FOR OUR HEALTH

NORMAN DANIELS, BRUCE KENNEDY,
AND ICHIRO KAWACHI

We have long known that the more affluent and better-educated members of a society tend to live longer and healthier lives: René Louis Villermé made this point as early as 1840, and it has been shown to hold for just about every human society. Recent research suggests that the correlations between income and health do not end there. We now know, for example, that countries with a greater degree of socioeconomic inequality show greater inequality in health status; also, that middle-income groups in relatively unequal societies have worse health than comparable, or even poorer, groups in more equal societies. Inequality, in short, seems to be bad for our health.

Moreover, and perhaps more surprisingly, universal access to health care does not necessarily break the link between social status and health. Our health is affected not simply by the ease with which we can see a doctor—though that surely matters—but also by our social position and the underlying inequality of our society. We cannot, of course,

infer causation from these correlations between social inequality and health inequality (though we will explore some
ideas about how the one might lead to the other). Suffice to
say that, while the exact processes are not fully understood,
the evidence suggests that there are *social determinants of
health*.

These social determinants offer a distinctive angle on
how to think about justice, public health, and reform of the
health care system. If social factors play a large role in deter-
mining our health, then efforts to ensure greater justice in
health care should not focus simply on the traditional health
sector. Health is produced not merely by having access to
medical prevention and treatment, but also, to a measurably
greater extent, by the cumulative experience of social conditions over the course of one's life. By the time a sixty-year-
old heart attack victim arrives at the emergency room,
bodily insults have accumulated over a lifetime. For such a
person, medical care is, figuratively speaking, "the ambu-
lance waiting at the bottom of the cliff." Much contemporary discussion about reducing health inequalities by increasing access to medical care misses this point. We should
be looking as well to improve social conditions—such as
access to basic education, levels of material deprivation,
a healthy workplace environment, and equality of political
participation—that help to determine the health of societies.

These conditions have unfortunately been virtually ignored within the academic field of bioethics, and in public discussions about health care reform. Academic bioethics is quick to focus on exotic new technologies and the vexing questions they raise for doctors and health administrators, who must make decisions about patient care and the allocation of scarce medical resources. And we all worry about the doctor-patient relationship under managed care, as insurance companies have taken a newly aggressive role in making medical decisions. But with some significant exceptions neither academic nor popular discussion has looked "upstream," past the new technologies, managed care, and the organization of health insurance, to the social arrangements that determine the health achievement of societies.

We hope to fill this gap by exploring some broader issues about health and social justice. To avoid vague generalities about justice, we shall advance a line of argument inspired principally by the theory of "justice as fairness" put forth by the philosopher John Rawls.[1] We find Rawls's theory compelling as an account of justice quite apart from its usefulness as an approach to the health care issue. But even those who do not share our ideas about justice may find our argument a helpful first step in thinking about social justice and public health.

Rawls's theory of justice as fairness was not designed to address issues of health care. He assumed a completely healthy population and argued that a just society must assure people equal basic liberties, guarantee that the right of political participation has roughly equal value for all, provide a robust form of equal opportunity, and limit inequalities to those that benefit the least advantaged. When these requirements of justice are met, Rawls argued, we can have reasonable confidence that others are showing us the respect that is essential to our sense of self-worth.

Recent empirical literature about the social determinants of health suggests that the failure to meet Rawlsian criteria for a just society is closely related to health inequality. The conjecture we propose to explore, then, is that by establishing equal liberties, robustly equal opportunity, a fair distribution of resources, and support for our self-respect—the basics of Rawlsian justice—we would go a long way toward eliminating the most important injustices in health outcomes. To be sure, social justice is valuable for reasons other than its effects on health. And social reform in the direction of greater justice would not eliminate the need to think hard about fair allocation of resources within the health care system. Still, acting to promote social justice may be a key step toward improving our health.

Social Determinants of Health

Let's take a closer look at some of the central findings in the recent literature on the social determinants of health, each of which has implications for an account of justice and health inequalities.

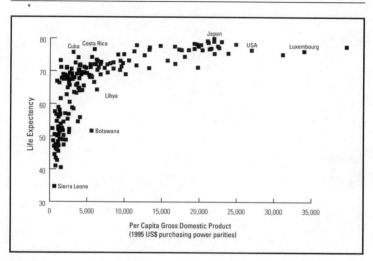

Figure 1: Relationship between country wealth and life expectancy, all nations

Cross-National Inequalities

A country's prosperity is related to its health, as measured, for example, by life expectancy: in richer countries people tend to live longer. This well-established finding suggests a natural ordering of societies along some fixed path of economic development: as a country or region develops economically, average health improves.

But the evidence suggests that things are more complicated. Figure 1 shows the relationship between the wealth of nations, as measured by per capita gross domestic product (GDPpc), and the health of nations, as measured by life expectancy. Clearly, GDPpc and life expectancy are closely as-

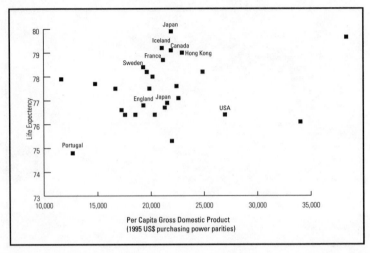

Figure 2: Wealth and life expectancy, countries with GDPpc over $10,000

sociated, but only up to a point. The relationship levels off when the GDPpc reaches $8,000 to $10,000; beyond this threshold, further economic advance buys virtually no further gains in life expectancy. This leveling effect is most apparent among the advanced industrial economies (see figure 2), which largely account for the upper tail of the curve in figure 1.

Closer inspection of these two figures shows some startling discrepancies. Though Cuba and Iraq are equally poor (each has a GDPpc of about $3,100), life expectancy in Cuba exceeds that in Iraq by 17.2 years. The difference between the GDPpc for Costa Rica and the United States is enormous (about $21,000), yet Costa Rica's life expectancy exceeds that of the United States (76.6 to 76.4). In fact, despite being the richest nation on the globe, the United States performs rather poorly on major health indicators.

Taken together, these observations show that the health of nations may depend, in part, on factors other than wealth. Culture, social organization, and government policies also help determine population health, and variations in these factors may explain many of the differences in health outcomes among nations.

Relative Income

One especially important factor in explaining the health of a society is the distribution of income: the health of a population depends not just on the size of the economic pie but on how the pie is shared. Differences in health outcomes among developed nations cannot be explained simply by the absolute deprivation associated with low economic development—lack of access to the basic material conditions necessary for health such as clean water, adequate nutrition and housing, and general sanitary living conditions. The degree of relative deprivation within a society also matters.

Numerous studies have provided support for this *relative-income hypothesis*, which states, more precisely, that inequality is strongly associated with population mortality and life expectancy across nations. To be sure, wealthier countries generally have higher average life expectancy. But rich countries, too, vary in life expectancy (see the tail of figure

1), and that variation dovetails with income distribution. Wealthy countries with more equal income distributions, such as Sweden and Japan, have higher life expectancies than does the United States, despite their having lower per capita GDP. Likewise, countries with a low GDPpc but remarkably high life expectancy, such as Costa Rica, tend to have a more equitable distribution of income.[2]

We find a similar pattern when we compare states within the United States. Wealthier states typically have lower mortality rates. But if we control for differences in state wealth, income inequality accounts for about 25 percent of the between-state variation in age-adjusted mortality rates. Furthermore, a recent study across U.S. metropolitan areas found that areas with high income inequality had an excess of death compared to areas with low inequality. This excess was very large, equivalent in magnitude to all deaths due to heart disease.[3]

Most of the evidence for this pattern comes from cross-sectional studies, which compare different places (countries, states, metropolitan areas) at a single point in time. But longitudinal studies, which look at a single place over time, support similar conclusions. Widening income differentials in both the United States and the United Kingdom have coincided with a slowing down of improvements in life expectancy. In many of the poorest areas of the United Kingdom, the mortality rate for several cohorts of relatively young people has increased as income inequality has widened. In the United States between 1980 and 1990, states with the highest income inequality showed slower rates of improvement in average life expectancy than did states with more equitable income distributions.[4]

Individual SES

Finally, when we move from comparing whole societies to comparing their individual members, we find, once more, that inequality is important. At the individual level, numerous studies have documented what has come to be known as the *socioeconomic gradient*: at each step along the socioeconomic ladder, we see improved health outcomes over the rung below. This suggests that differences in health outcomes are not confined to the extremes of rich and poor but are observed across all levels of socioeconomic status (SES).[5]

Moreover, the SES gradient does not appear to be explained by differences in access to health care. Steep gradients have been observed even among groups of individuals, such as British civil servants, who all have adequate access to health care, housing, and transport.[6]

The slope of the gradient varies substantially across societies. Some societies show a relatively shallow gradient in mortality rates: being better off confers a health advantage, but not so large an advantage as elsewhere. Others, with comparable or even higher levels of economic development, show much steeper gradients. The slope of the gradient appears to be fixed by the level of income inequality in a society: the more unequal a society is in economic terms, the more unequal it is in health terms. Moreover, middle-income groups in a country with high income inequality typically do worse in terms of health than comparable or even poorer groups in a society with less income inequality. We find the same pattern within the United States when we examine state and metropolitan area variations in inequality and health outcomes.[7]

Pathways

Earlier, we cautioned that correlations between inequality and health do not necessarily imply causation. Still, there are plausible and identifiable pathways through which social inequalities appear to produce health inequalities. In the United States, the states with the most unequal income distributions invest less in public education, have larger uninsured populations, and spend less on social safety nets. The facts on educational spending and educational outcomes are especially striking: controlling for median income, income inequality explains about 40 percent of the variation between states in the percentage of children in the fourth grade who are below the basic reading level. Similarly strong associations are seen for high school dropout rates. It is evident from these data that educational opportunities for children in high-income-inequality states are quite different from those in states with more egalitarian distributions. These effects on education have an immediate impact on health, increasing the likelihood of premature death during childhood and adolescence (as evidenced by the much higher death rates for infants and children in the high-inequality states). Later in life, they appear in the SES gradient in health.

When we compare countries, we also find that differential investment in human capital—in particular, education—is a strong predictor of health. Indeed, one of the strongest predictors of life expectancy among developing countries is adult literacy, particularly the disparity between male and female adult literacy, which explains much of the variation in health achievement among these countries after accounting for GDPpc. For example, among the 125 developing countries with a GDPpc less than $10,000, the difference between male and female literacy accounts for 40 percent of the variation in life expectancy after factoring out the effect of the GDPpc. The fact that gender disparities in access to basic education drive the level of health achievement further underscores the role of broader social inequalities in patterning health inequalities. Indeed, in the United States, differences between the states in women's status—measured in terms of their economic autonomy and political participation—are strongly negatively correlated with female mortality rates: higher status is associated with lower mortality.

These societal mechanisms—for example, income inequality leading to educational inequality leading to health inequality—are tightly linked to the political processes that influence government policy. For example, income inequality appears to affect health by undermining civil society. Income inequality erodes social cohesion, as indicated by higher levels of social mistrust and reduced participation in civic organizations. Lack of social cohesion leads to lower participation in political activity (such as voting, serving in local government, volunteering for political campaigns). And lower participation, in turn, undermines the responsiveness of government institutions in addressing the needs of the worst off. States with the highest income inequality, and thus lowest levels of social capital and political participation, are less likely to invest in human capital and provide far less generous social safety nets.[8]

In short, the case for social determinants of health is strong. What are the implications of this fact for ideas of justice?

INEQUALITIES AND INEQUITIES

When is a health inequality between two groups "inequitable"? Margaret Whitehead and Goran Dahlgren have suggested a useful and influential answer: health inequalities count as inequities when they are avoidable, unnecessary, and unfair.[9]

The Whitehead/Dahlgren analysis is deliberately broad. Age, gender, race, and ethnic differences in health status exist independent of the socioeconomic differences we have been discussing, and they raise distinct questions about equity. For example, should we view the lower life expectancy of men compared to women in developed countries as an inequity? If it is rooted in biological differences that we do not know how to overcome, then it is unavoidable (and therefore not an inequity). This is not an idle controversy: taking average, rather than gender-differentiated, life expectancy in developed countries as a benchmark will yield different estimates of the degree of inequity women face in some developing countries. In any case, the analysis of inequity is only as good as our understanding of what is avoidable or unnecessary.

The same point applies to judgments about fairness. Is the poorer health status of groups whose members smoke and drink heavily unfair? We may be inclined to say it is not unfair, provided that participation in such risky behaviors is truly voluntary. But if many people in a cultural group or class behave similarly, then the behavior might acquire the qualities of a social norm—in which case we might wonder just how voluntary the behavior is (and therefore how much responsibility we should ascribe to them for it). Whitehead and Dahlgren's terms leave us with an unresolved complexity of judgments about responsibility, and as a result, with disagreements about fairness and avoidability.

The poor in many countries lack access to clean water, sanitation, adequate shelter, basic education, vaccinations, and prenatal and maternal care. As a result of some, or all, of these factors, infant mortality rates for the poor exceed those for the rich. Since social policies could supply the missing determinants of infant health, these inequalities are avoidable.

Are these inequalities also unfair? Most of us would think they are, perhaps because we believe that policies that create and sustain poverty are unjust, and perhaps also because we object to social policies that compound economic poverty with lack of access to the determinants of health. The problem of justice in health care becomes more complicated, however, when we remember one of the basic findings from the literature on social determinants: we cannot eliminate health inequalities simply by eliminating poverty. Health inequalities persist even in societies that provide the poor with access to all standard public health and medical services, as well as basic income and education, and they persist as a gradient of health throughout the social hierarchy, not just between the very poorest groups and those above them.

What, then, are we to think of the health inequalities that would persist, even if poverty were eliminated? To eliminate health inequalities, should we eliminate all socioeconomic inequalities? We might believe that all socioeconomic inequalities, or at least all inequalities we did not freely choose, are unjust—but very few embrace such a radical egalitarian view. Indeed, we may well believe that some degree of socioeconomic inequality is unavoidable, or even necessary, and therefore not unjust. On issues of this kind, we should take guidance from a well-articulated account of social justice—the one put forth by John Rawls.

Justice as Fairness

In *A Theory of Justice*, Rawls sought to show that a social contract designed to be fair to free and equal people would lead to equal basic liberties and equal opportunity and would permit inequalities only when they work to make the worst-off groups fare as well as possible. Though Rawls's account was devised for the most general questions of social justice, it also provides a set of principles for the just distribution of the social determinants of health.

Rawls did not talk about disease or health in his original account. To simplify the construction of his theory, he assumed that his contractors were fully functional over a normal life span—no one becomes ill or dies prematurely. This idealization provides a clue about how to extend this theory to the real world of illness and premature death. The goal of public health and medicine is to keep people as close to the idealization of normal functioning as possible under reasonable resource constraints. Maintaining normal functioning, in turn, makes a limited but significant contribution to protecting the range of opportunities open to individuals. So one might see the distribution of health care as governed by a norm of fair equality of opportunity.

We can now say more directly why justice, as described by Rawls's principles, is good for our health.

Let us start by considering what a just society would require with regard to the distribution of the social determinants of health. In such an ideal society, everyone is guaranteed equal basic liberties, including the right to participate in politics. In addition, there are safeguards aimed at assuring for all, whether richer or poorer, the worth or value of those rights. Since, as we argued above, there is evidence that political participation is a social determinant of health, the Rawlsian ideal assures institutional protections that counter the usual effects of socioeconomic inequalities on participation—and thus on health.

Moreover, according to Rawls, justice requires fair equality of opportunity. This principle condemns discriminatory barriers and requires robust measures aimed at mitigating the effects of socioeconomic inequalities and other contingencies on opportunity. In addition to equitable public education, such measures would include the provision of developmentally appropriate day care and early childhood interventions intended to promote the development of capabilities independently of the advantages of family background. These measures match, or go beyond, the best models of equal-opportunity interventions currently in place, such as European efforts at day care and early childhood education. We also note that the strategic importance of education for protecting equal opportunity has implications for all levels of education, including access to graduate and professional education.

The equal opportunity principle also requires extensive public health, medical, and social support services aimed at promoting normal functioning for all. It even provides a rationale for the social costs of reasonable accommodation to incurable disabilities, as required by the Americans with Disabilities Act. Because the equal opportunity principle aims at promoting normal functioning for all as a way of protecting opportunity for all, it at once aims at improving population health and reducing health inequalities. Obviously, this focus requires provision of universal access to comprehensive health care, including public health, primary health care, and medical and social support services.

To act justly in health policy, we must have knowledge about the causal pathways through which socioeconomic (and other) inequalities work to produce differential health outcomes. Suppose we learn, for example, that workplace organization induces stress and a loss of control, and that these tend, in turn, to promote health inequalities. We should then think of modifying those features of workplace organization in order to mitigate their negative effects on health as a public health requirement of the equal opportunity approach.

Finally, a just society restricts inequalities in income and wealth to those that benefit the least advantaged. Rawls calls this requirement the "difference principle." The inequalities allowed by this principle—in conjunction with the principles assuring equal opportunity and the value of political participation—are probably more constrained than those we observe in even the most industrialized societies. If so, just inequalities would produce a flatter gradient of health inequality than we currently observe in even the more extensive welfare systems of northern Europe.

In short, Rawlsian justice—though not devised for the case of health—regulates the distribution of the key social determinants of health, including the social bases of self-respect. There is nothing about the theory that should make us focus narrowly on medical services. Properly understood, justice as fairness tells us what justice requires in the distribution of all socially controllable determinants of health.

We still face a theoretical issue of some interest. Even if a just distribution of the determinants of health flattens health gradients further than what we observe in the most egalitarian developed countries, we must still expect a residue of health inequalities: people who are less well off in economic terms will continue to be less healthy. Should we aim to reduce further those otherwise justifiable economic inequalities because of the inequalities in health status they create?

Suppose we reduce socioeconomic inequalities and thereby reduce health inequalities—but the result is that the health of all is worsened because productivity is reduced so much that important institutions are undermined. That is not acceptable. Our commitment to reducing health inequality should not require steps that threaten to make health worse off for those with less-than-equal health status. So the theoretical issue reduces to this: would it ever be reasonable to allow some health inequality in order to produce some nonhealth benefits for those with the worst health prospects?

We know that in real life people routinely trade health risks for other benefits. They do so when they commute longer distances for a better job or take a ski vacation. Trades of this kind raise questions of fairness. For example, when is hazard pay a benefit workers gain only because their opportunities are unfairly restricted? When is it an appropriate exercise of their autonomy? Some such trades are unfair; others will be restricted only by paternalists.

Rawls gave priority to the principle of protecting equal basic liberties because he believed that once people achieve some threshold level of material well-being, they will not trade fundamental liberties for other goods. Making such a trade might deny them the liberty to pursue their most cherished ideals, including their religious beliefs, whatever they turn out to be. Can we make the same argument about trading health for other goods?

There is some plausibility to the claim that rational people should refrain from trading their health for other goods. Loss of health may preclude us from pursuing what we most value in life. We do, after all, see people willing to trade almost anything to regain health once they lose it.

Nevertheless, there is also strong reason to think this priority is not clear-cut, especially when the trade is between a risk to health and other goods that people highly value. Refusing to allow any (*ex ante*) trades of health risks for other goods, even when the background conditions on choice are otherwise fair, may seem unjustifiably paternalistic, perhaps in a way that a refusal to allow trades of basic liberties is not.

We propose a pragmatic route around this problem. Fair equality of opportunity is only approximated even in an ideally just system, because we can only mitigate, not eliminate, the effects of family and other social contingencies. For example, only if we were willing to violate widely respected parental liberties could we intrude into family life and "rescue" children from parental values that arguably interfere with equal opportunity. Similarly, though we give a general priority to equal opportunity over the difference principle, we cannot achieve complete equality in health any more than we can achieve completely equal opportunity. Justice is always rough around the edges.

Suppose, then, that the decision about trade-offs is made by the legislature in a democratic society in which everyone has a fair chance to participate. Because those principles require effective political participation across all socioeconomic groups, we can suppose that groups most directly affected by any trade-off decision have a voice in the decision. Since there is a residual health gradient, groups affected by the trade-off include not only the worst off, but those in the middle as well. A democratic process that involved deliberation about the trade-off and its effects might be the best we could do to provide a resolution of the unanswered theoretical question.

In contrast, where the fair value of political participation is not adequately assured—and we doubt it is so assured in even our most democratic societies—we have much less confidence in the fairness of a democratic decision about how to trade health against other goods. It is much more likely under actual conditions that those who benefit most from the inequalities—that is, those who are better off— also wield disproportionate political power and will influence decisions about trade-offs to serve their interests. It may still be that the use of a democratic process in nonideal conditions is the fairest resolution we can practically achieve, but it still falls well short of what an ideally just democratic process involves.

If we were to achieve a just distribution of resources, then, with the least well off being as well off as possible, there would still be health inequalities. But decisions about whether to reduce those inequalities even more are matters for democratic process. Justice itself does not command their reduction.

Policy Implications

We earlier suggested that the Whitehead/Dahlgren analysis of health inequities (inequalities that are avoidable and unfair) is useful. We then suggested that the Rawlsian account of justice as fairness provides a fuller account of what is fair and unfair in the distribution of the social determinants of health. The theory provides a more systematic way to think about which health inequalities are inequities. And it delivers the conclusion that most health inequalities that we now observe worldwide among socioeconomic and racial or ethnic groups are "inequities" that should be remedied. Even the countries with the shallowest health gradients, such as Sweden and England, have viewed their own health inequalities as unacceptable and have initiated policy measures to mitigate them. Clearly, the broader World Health Organization efforts in this direction are, probably without exception, also aimed at true inequities.

Before saying more about the kind of reforms outside the health care system that would improve our health, we want to head off a misconception. We are not suggesting that we should simply ignore medical services and health sector reform because other steps will have a bigger long-term health payoff. Even if we had a highly just distribution of the social determinants of health and of public health measures, people will still become ill and need medical services. The fair design of a health system arguably should give some extra weight to meeting actual medical needs.

To see the importance of meeting medical needs, let's distinguish between "identified victims"—people who are already ill and have known needs—and "statistical victims," whose lives would be spared illness by robust public health measures and a fairer distribution of social determinants of health. We might be tempted to judge these lives impartially, to say that statistical lives saved are just as valuable or important as identified victims. But other considerations temper our inclination to such impartial reallocation from identified to statistical victims and suggest that we give special moral weight to the urgent needs of those already ill. Medical providers may legitimately believe that the good they can control through their delivery of medical care has a greater claim on them than the good that would be brought about by more indirect measures beyond their control. More generally, many of us will be connected as family members and friends to the identified victims and will feel that we have obligations to assist them that supersede the obligations we have to more distant, statistical victims.

We do not suggest, then, that our society should immediately reallocate resources away from medicine to schools, for example, in the hope and expectation that a better-educated population will be healthier. But the arguments here suggest that some reallocations of resources to improve the social determinants are justifiable.

Domestic Policy

What sorts of social policies should governments pursue to reduce health inequalities? The menu of options ought to include policies aimed at equalizing individual life opportunities, such as investment in basic education, affordable housing, income security, and other forms of antipoverty policy. Though the connection between these social policies and health may seem somewhat remote, and they are rarely linked to issues of health in our public policy discussions, the evidence outlined earlier suggests that they should be part of the debate. The kinds of policies suggested by a social determinants perspective encompass a much broader range of instruments than would ordinarily be considered for improving the health of the population.

Consider, then, four examples of social policies that might improve health by reducing socioeconomic disparities: investment in early childhood development, nutrition programs, improvements in the quality of the work environment, and reductions in income inequality.

1. Early Life Intervention. Growing evidence points to the importance of early childhood environment in influencing the behavior, learning, and health of individuals later in the life course. Ensuring equal opportunity requires interventions as early in life as possible. Several studies have demonstrated the benefits of early supportive environments for children. In the Perry High/Scope Project, children in poor economic circumstances were provided a high-quality early childhood development program between the ages of three and five. Compared to a control group, those in the intervention group completed more schooling by age twenty-seven; were more likely to be employed, own a home, and be married with children; experienced fewer criminal problems and teenage pregnancies; and were far less likely to have mental health problems.

Compensatory education and nutrition in the early years of life seem also to yield important gains for the most disadvantaged groups. As part of the War on Poverty, the federal government introduced two small compensatory education programs: Head Start for preschoolers and Chapter 1 for elementary school children. Evaluations of these programs indicate that children who enroll in them learn more than those who do not. So the programs create more equality of opportunity. Educational achievement, meanwhile, is a powerful predictor of health in later life, partly because education provides access to employment and income and partly because education has a direct influence on health behavior in adulthood, including diet, smoking, and physical activity. So the programs also lead to more health equality.

2. Nutrition. A similarly persuasive case can be made for nutritional supplementation in low-income women and children. An analysis of the National Maternal and Infant Health Survey found that participation of low-income pregnant women in the WIC program (the Special Supplemental Nutrition Program for Women, Infants, and Children) was associated with about a 40 percent reduction in the risk of subsequent infant death. A mother's nutritional state affects her infant's chance of death not just in the first year of life but also throughout the life course. Thus a woman's weight prior to pregnancy is one of the strongest predictors of her child's birth weight; in turn, low birth weight has been shown to be linked with increased risks of coronary heart disease, hypertension, and diabetes in later life. It follows that investing in policies that reduce early adverse influences may produce benefits not only in the present but also for future generations.

3. Work Environment. We alluded earlier to the finding that the health status of workers is closely linked to the quality of their work environment, specifically to the amount of control and autonomy available to workers on their jobs. Low-control work environments—such as monotonous machine-paced work (e.g., factory assembly lines) or jobs involving little opportunity for learning and utilization of new skills (e.g., supermarket cashiers)—tend to be concentrated among low-income occupations. Michael Marmot and colleagues have shown that social disparities in health arise partly as a consequence of the way labor markets sort individuals into positions of unequal authority and control. Low-control, highly demanding job conditions not only are more common in lower-status occupations but also place workers at increased risks of hypertension, cardiovascular disease, mental illness, musculoskeletal disease, and physical disability.

A growing number of case studies from around the world have concluded that it is possible to improve the level of control in workplaces by several means: increasing the variety of different tasks in the production process, encouraging workforce participation in the production process, and allowing more flexible work arrangements, such as altering the patterns of shift work to make them less disruptive of workers' lives. In some cases it may even be possible to redesign the workplace and to enhance worker autonomy without adversely affecting productivity, since absence due to sickness may diminish as a consequence of a healthier workplace.

4. Income Redistribution. Many policies suggested by the social determinants perspective tend to fall under the category of antipoverty policy. However, research on the social determinants of health warns us that antipoverty policies do not go far enough in reducing unjust health disparities. Though priority should go to reducing the plight of the worst off, the fact is that health inequalities occur as a gradient: the poor have worse health than the near-poor, but the near-poor fare worse than the lower middle class, the lower middle class do worse than the upper middle class, and so on up the economic ladder. Addressing the social gradient in health requires action above and beyond the elimination of poverty.

To address comprehensively the problem of health inequalities, governments must begin to address the issue of economic inequalities directly. Evidence we sketched earlier indicates that the extent of socioeconomic disparities—the size of the gap in incomes and assets between the top and bottom of society—is itself an important determinant of the health achievement of society, independent of the average standard of living. Most important, economic disparities seem to influence the degree of equality in measures of political participation, including voting, campaign donations, contacting elected officials, and other forms of political activity. The more unequal the distribution of incomes and assets, the more skewed the patterns of political participation, and consequently, the greater the degree of political exclusion of disadvantaged groups.

Inequalities in political participation determine the kinds of policies passed by national and local governments. For example, Kim Hill and colleagues studied the relationship between the degree of electoral mobilization of lower-class voters and the generosity of welfare benefits provided by state governments. Even after adjusting for other factors that might predict state welfare policy—the degree of public liberalism in the state, the federal government's welfare cost-matching rate for individual states, the state unemployment rate and median income, and state taxes—robust relationships were found between the extent of political participation by lower-class voters and the degree of generosity of state welfare payments. In other words, who participates matters for political outcomes, and the resulting policies have an important impact on the opportunities for the poor to lead a healthy life.

For both of the foregoing reasons—that it yields a higher level of health achievement as well as greater political participation—the reduction of income inequality ought to be a priority of governments concerned about addressing social inequalities in health. Although discussion of strategies is beyond our scope here, a number of levers do exist by which governments could address the problem of income inequality, spanning from the radical (a commitment to sustained full employment, collective wage bargaining, and progressive taxation) to the incremental (expansion of the earned income tax credit, increased child care credit, and raising the minimum wage).

International Development

Our discussion has implications for international development theory, as well as for economic choices confronted by industrialized countries. To the extent that income distribution matters for population health status, it is not obvious that giving strict priority to economic growth is the optimal strategy for maximizing social welfare. Raising everyone's income will improve the health status of the poor—the trickle-down approach—but not as much as paying attention to the distribution of the social product would. Within the developing world, a comparison of Kerala, a state in India, with highly unequal countries such as Brazil and South Africa illustrates this point. Despite having only one-third to a quarter of the income of Brazil or South Africa (and thereby having a higher prevalence of poverty in the absolute sense), the citizens of Kerala nonetheless live longer, most likely as a result of the higher priority that the government of Kerala accords to a fair distribution of economic gains.

The real issue for developing countries is what kind of

economic growth is salutary. Hence Jean Dreze and Amartya Sen distinguish between two types of successes in the rapid reduction of mortality, which they term "growth-mediated" and "support-led" processes. The former works mainly through fast economic growth, exemplified by mortality reductions in countries such as South Korea or Hong Kong. Their successes depended on the growth process being wide-based and participatory (for example, full employment policies) and on the gains from economic growth being utilized to expand social services in the public sector, particularly health care and education. Their experiences stand in stark contrast to the example of countries such as Brazil, which have similarly achieved rapid economic growth but have lagged behind in health improvements.

In contrast to growth-mediated processes, "support-led" processes—for example, in China, Costa Rica, or Kerala—operate not through fast economic growth but through governments giving high priority to the provision of social services that reduce mortality and enhance the quality of life.

Policies of either kind can succeed in promoting the health of the population. In either case, success depends on generating a more fair distribution of income. Once more, health is the by-product of justice.

We noted earlier that academic bioethics and popular discussion of health care reform have generally tended to focus on medicine at the point of delivery and have inadequately attended to determinants of health "upstream" from the medical system itself. Empirical findings about the social determinants of health suggest that this is a serious mistake: upstream is precisely where we need to look. Put these findings together with a philosophical theory of justice that might apply to any society, and we get this striking result: In a just society, health inequalities will be minimized and population health status will be improved—in short, social justice is good for our health.[10]

2

DO INEQUALITIES MATTER?

MICHAEL MARMOT

Do inequalities in health matter? Have we not reached the end of history as far as health in the rich countries of the world, members of the Organization of Economic Cooperation and Development (OECD), is concerned? My answer to both questions, like that of Daniels and colleagues, is that inequalities in health do matter and that we have not reached the end of history. Dramatic as have been the advances in health this century in OECD countries, there is still a way to go. Taking the simplest summary measure, life expectancy at birth, the United States is in the bottom half of the rich countries.

In fact, the answer to these two questions may be linked. One reason countries have failed to reach their full health potential is persisting inequalities in health. It has been known for years that there are pockets of extreme deprivation and poor life expectancy within rich countries. In Harlem, for example, life expectancy for young men is lower than for young men in Bangladesh. Furthermore, as Daniels and colleagues emphasize, the problem in rich countries is not one of poor health for the deprived and good health for the nondeprived but one of a social gradient in health. In the

Whitehall studies of British civil servants—white-collar workers in stable jobs—there was a step-wise relation between grade of employment and ill health: the lower the grade the higher the rate of morbidity and mortality. These findings are typical of those from national figures.

The slope of the ill-health gradient varies over time within countries and between countries. The fact that it is not a fixed property of society suggests that it is potentially changeable.

There are, then, at least three reasons to be concerned about inequalities in health: pragmatic reasons, ethical reasons, and social reasons (what inequalities in health may reflect about the wider society). In practice, the distinction between these may be less than might first appear. First, the pragmatic issue: Daniels, Kennedy, and Kawachi refer to evidence that in those countries where health inequalities are greatest, overall health status of the population is lower. It is difficult to lower the coronary heart disease mortality of the population if only part of the population is experiencing improvement.

Second, inequalities in health that are potentially avoidable are unfair. Margaret Thatcher famously asserted that there is no such thing as society. The rest of us, who think there is, may feel that social justice is a reason for desiring a reduction in social inequalities in health.

Third, and this is at the heart of the authors' argument, if health is a reflection of wider social influences, then health inequalities are a reflection of inequalities in society. One might complain that this is not a sufficient answer to the question of why we should be concerned with health inequalities: it merely shifts the question further back.

Why, then, should we be concerned with inequalities in society? One could imagine an argument that went as follows: Americans think that economic inequalities are a good thing because they reflect economic freedoms that are essential for wealth creation; they think that social safety nets are a bad thing in principle. Therefore, the type of society people want is one characterized by high inequalities of income and wealth and little spending on social safety nets. If health inequalities happen to follow from such a set of social arrangements, that is unfortunate but not of central concern. (Writing from Britain, I am a poor judge of what Americans think, but it is possible that this reflects a prevalent view among the relatively small proportion of people who actually vote in elections, if not among the large proportion, for a democracy, who do not.)

The authors appeal to Rawls's theory of justice to argue that such a society is not just, because it does not establish "equal liberties, robustly equal opportunity, a fair distribution of resources, and support for our self-respect." They argue that a just society would go a long way toward eliminating the most important injustices in health outcomes. I agree with their conclusions that therefore priority should be given to early life intervention, ensuring adequate nutrition to those least able to afford it, improving work environments, and redistributing income.

I am too much influenced by the writing of Amartya Sen, however, to accept the appeal to Rawls without a quibble, one that may seem minor given that I accept the conclusions the authors seem to have reached on the basis of their Rawlsian analysis. Sen argues that any ethical social system requires equality of something. The question is, what? (Or, as Sen might put it, in which space is inequality to be measured?) Equality of economic freedoms is one such space; equality of basic liberties, as in Rawls, is another. How to choose between these different notions of equality? One way is with regard to their consequences, such as health. Some philosophers coin rude words like *consequentialist* to describe those who are concerned about consequences. But Sen, critical of Rawls because of what he considered an insufficient concern with outcomes, suggested a different evaluative framework for assessing inequality—one that took account of its impact on our capability and freedom to lead the lives we want to lead.

I suspect that there is the basis for important philosophical disagreement here that perhaps need not detain us at the moment. Even if Daniels and colleagues do not explicitly share Sen's concern with the consequences of Rawlsian justice, they are nevertheless deeply concerned with health inequalities. Their argument is a strong one. Concern with social inequality follows from Rawlsian analysis. That this leads Daniels, Kennedy, and Kawachi to be concerned with the social determinants of health and to make recommendations that would lead to the reduction of health inequalities is all to the good.

POCKETS OF POVERTY

MARCIA ANGELL

Daniels, Kennedy, and Kawachi have written an important and deeply humane essay. They take as their starting point the well-known observation that wealthier populations are on average healthier and that the more evenly wealth is distributed within a population, the better the average health. Thus, life expectancy in rich countries is higher than in poor countries, and it is higher in countries like Sweden, where wealth is spread relatively evenly, than it is in similarly rich countries, such as the United States, where there are vast disparities. The authors conclude, reasonably enough, that there are social determinants of health and that these determinants vary across and within populations. Less reasonably, they conclude that there is something about inequality itself, quite apart from poverty, that is a risk to health. On this basis, they propose that lessening income disparities within populations would improve the overall health of a population. Their philosophical underpinning is Rawls's theory of justice, but that is hardly necessary for the case that the reforms they suggest would make the United States a healthier, wiser, and more decent nation. There is no question that socioeconomic status and health are tightly linked, and the effect of one on the other can be huge. For example, in a study of the use of aspirin to prevent heart attacks in male physicians, the modest benefit of aspirin was swamped by the benefits apparently conferred by the high socioeconomic status of these men. The overall rate of fatal heart attacks in the physicians was only 12 percent of what would be expected in men from the general population. (To be sure, we don't know whether doctors might do better than other privileged groups, such as lawyers, because of their medical education, but even if that were true, medical education would still have to be counted as a social determinant.) Very few medicines or interventions can offer such a benefit.

Indeed, the fact that social advantage correlates so closely and powerfully with health can make it extremely difficult to interpret the results of clinical research. Studies of the effect of passive smoking on childhood asthma, for example, are impossible to interpret unless they attempt to control for socioeconomic status. Without such control, it is impossible to know whether the increased prevalence of asthma in the children of smokers is really because of passive smoking or because smokers are more likely to be poor and poverty itself is associated with asthma for other reasons. Similarly, studies of the effect of lead exposure on intelligence are confounded by socioeconomic status. The children of well-educated parents are more likely to do well on IQ tests and are also less likely to be exposed to lead. It is hard to know, then, what causes low IQ scores: lead or lack of parental education.

Yet, despite the undoubted importance of socioeconomic

status to health, no one knows which aspect of social standing matters—wealth or education or occupation or some other condition—much less how it operates. We are dealing here with a black box—the most mysterious and powerful of all determinants of health. Differences in medical care seem to account for only a small part of the effect, as pointed out by Daniels, Kennedy, and Kawachi. The lion's share of the effect is caused by other factors, mostly unknown. Since it is inconceivable that money in the bank or a sheepskin on the wall could directly affect health, they must be markers for the real factors that matter.

What might those factors be? Most good studies of the subject—and there are lamentably few—try to control for the usual suspects, such as cigarette smoking and heavy drinking, both of which are more frequent among people of lower socioeconomic status. Even after controlling for them, the health disparities across social strata persist, although they are lessened. The increased frequencies of trauma, substance abuse, and HIV infection among the disadvantaged cannot explain the differences, either, since death rates from other causes, such as heart disease and cancer, are also higher in poor people. One can imagine a host of influences that might affect health—such as diet, stress, exposure to infectious agents or toxins—that are related to socioeconomic status, but there is very little evidence to point to any of them as a major cause of the health disparities across income groups.

Some people suggest that in analyzing the association between health and socioeconomic status, we tend to confuse cause and effect. They believe that privilege does not lead to better health, but rather the reverse—healthier people tend to become richer and better educated because they are more energetic and competitive. A variation of this view holds that both health and wealth stem from good genes. Whatever the answer to the question of why socioeconomic status is correlated with health, the question deserves serious study. Good research in this area will undoubtedly yield enormous dividends in understanding human biology and health, and Daniels, Kennedy, and Kawachi are on solid ground in pointing us in that direction.

They are on less solid ground in their contention that inequality somehow contributes to poor health directly, above and beyond the effects of poverty itself. Although there is some evidence of that from international comparisons, it is by no means consistent. Denmark, for example, has about the same per capita wealth as the United States with less inequality, but its life expectancy is lower. Kerala and Costa Rica, which provide the strongest support for a direct benefit of equality, are such outliers that it is risky to generalize from them.

Unequal societies, by definition, have pockets of poverty and pockets of great wealth. If the pockets of poverty contribute disproportionately to population measures of health

—such as average life expectancy—that would explain the apparent correlation between inequality and poor health. I believe that is the likely explanation. Inequality just *seems* to be a direct contributor to poor health, whereas the real cause is poverty. Daniels, Kennedy, and Kawachi base their argument for a direct effect of inequality on the notion of a linear health gradient that operates equally across all socioeconomic strata, so that the wealthy benefit as much as the poor lose. But the evidence for that is weak. There have not been sufficient studies of a broad enough range of income levels to know what the shape of the curve is. The best information may come from international comparisons showing that with increasing wealth the health benefits become smaller and smaller until a plateau is reached.

One need not invoke some mysterious effect of inequality on health to make a very strong argument for lessening inequalities that lead to deprivation at the low end of the scale. Poverty is crippling not only physically but intellectually and spiritually. It cripples any wealthy society that tolerates it on a large scale, as does the United States. In addition to the loss of human potential and the social pathology that grows out of poverty, the costs include the callousness that inures the rest of society to its presence, even as many people enjoy extraordinary riches.

The fact that there are also health consequences of poverty, whether they are exacerbated by inequality or not, is doubly punishing and adds greatly to the injustice. Daniels,

Kennedy, and Kawachi are right about that. F. Scott Fitz-
gerald famously pointed out that the rich are different from
the rest of us. But what is less well known is that he observed
that no difference that divides people is so important as that
between the well and the sick. I agree.

EQUAL OPPORTUNITY

SUDHIR ANAND AND FABIENNE PETER

In the field of public health it is common knowledge that the determinants of people's health include many factors other than medical care. In the same vein, the contemporary literature on social inequalities in health has stressed the importance of social factors other than access to health care. It is thus surprising that bioethics has, until recently, focused exclusively on medical care and neglected the ethical implications of broader social factors that impact people's health. The good news is that this is changing, and there is now significant ongoing work on the topic of health equity. The essay by Daniels, Kennedy, and Kawachi is an example. We agree with the authors that social inequalities in health raise important questions about justice, but have some comments on the details of their argument.

Daniels, Kennedy, and Kawachi define social inequalities in health as differences in average health between socioeconomic groups. If we are concerned about social justice, however, this definition does not go far enough. The empirical literature shows significant health differentials with respect to other social groups too—for instance, those defined by gender, race and ethnicity, or geographical location. The problem is compounded if these factors interact with socioeconomic status, and as a result, health differentials exist *within* socioeconomic groups—for example, black men with low incomes have worse health than white men with similar incomes.

The authors use the framework developed by Margaret Whitehead and Goran Dahlgren to link empirical research on social inequalities in health with philosophical work on justice. According to Whitehead and Dahlgren, inequalities in health are inequitable (unjust) if they are "avoidable, unnecessary, and unfair." Yet, fairness surely subsumes what is unavoidable and what is "necessary." Problems of justice and fairness arise only if a certain outcome could have been otherwise; and if what is necessary is interpreted to mean something other than what is unavoidable, then a judgment on what is necessary must ultimately be made with reference to justice and fairness. The framework thus reduces to the question: when are health inequalities unfair or unjust, and why?

The authors base their response on Rawls's theory of justice as fairness. The issue is whether the existing framework of Rawlsian justice can take care of the problem of social inequalities in health, or whether we need to rethink what justice requires in addressing health inequalities. The authors do not settle this issue, and two different views of the relationship between Rawlsian justice and social inequalities in health are identifiable in their paper.

The first view is that although Rawls did not have the

problem of social inequalities in health in mind when he formulated his conception of justice as fairness, implementing his principles will go a long way toward reducing such inequalities. This argument suggests that we do not need to pay special attention to the problem of health inequalities. By ensuring greater justice in Rawls's original sense, we will—as a side effect—also solve the problem of health inequalities. This view relies on the premise—not made explicit by the authors—that inequalities in health are unjust if, and only if, they are the result of unjust social arrangements.

The second view is based on the premise that a conception of justice should explicitly tackle problems of inequalities in health. This view relies on an extension of the Rawlsian principle of "fair equality of opportunity." Daniels originally developed this view in his book *Just Health Care* to deal with fair access to health care. According to this account, health is defined as normal functioning, and fair equality of opportunity requires the maintenance of normal functioning. But if broader social factors affect people's health, there is no reason why the extension of the principle of fair equality of opportunity should apply only to health care and neglect the other determinants of health.

We thus discern two views as to how Rawlsian justice might apply in dealing with the problem of social inequalities in health. Their simultaneous presence in the essay creates a tension, since they each might yield a different assessment of what should be done and for what reason. Whereas the extended fair equality of opportunity principle seems to require efforts to correct health inequalities as such, the first account addresses the problem only indirectly. Moreover, the first account is contingent on the empirical relationships that Kawachi, Kennedy, and others have observed. Had the empirical relationships observed been the reverse—for example, had higher income inequality been associated with smaller health inequalities—then implementing Rawlsian justice according to the first view could actually worsen inequalities in health. On the other hand, the extended fair equality of opportunity view is not contingent on any such empirical relationships and appears to provide a stand-alone case for redressing social inequalities in health.

The tension becomes even more apparent when the authors consider whether we should correct those social inequalities in health that remain after we have implemented Rawlsian justice according to the first view. Specifically, they ask whether it would ever be "reasonable to allow some health inequality in order to produce some nonhealth benefits for those with the worst health prospects." If trade-offs between health and nonhealth goods are admissible, these health inequalities may be justifiable—provided the nonhealth gains under just social arrangements compensate for the health losses. The authors suggest that decisions about trade-offs and compensation are matters for the democratic process and not for justice itself to settle. But what if pervasive inequalities in health remain—or are even exacerbated—with or without compensation through other goods? What is needed, it seems to us, is an account that explicitly evaluates the distribution of health outcomes and recognizes that health inequalities raise independent problems of social justice. The extended fair equality of opportunity principle would appear to provide the basis for such an account. Were the authors to develop this account, though, the first view of what Rawlsian justice requires would seem to be redundant.

Recent research on social inequalities in health does raise important questions about justice, and in principle we have no problem with the use of a Rawlsian approach. To us, however, the account provided by Daniels, Kennedy, and Kawachi remains ambiguous about the precise conception of justice that is invoked to address the problem of social inequalities in health.

POLICY OPTIONS

TED MARMOR

The article by Daniels, Kennedy, and Kawachi promises far more, I am afraid, than it delivers. This is all the more disappointing since I applaud the effort to join empirical analysis of health and health care to normative disputes about what public policies should be enacted and realistic discussions of what policies can be implemented. My reservations fall into two categories. First, I am concerned about the authors' basic claim that inequality *per se* is "bad for our health." Second, I am not convinced that, even assuming income inequalities cause significant health inequalities, justice requires more effort to reduce income differences than to make access to medical care more equal. In that connection, I raise questions about the general presumption that discovering causal pathways in social arrangements leads directly to what the authors call "policy implications."

Before proceeding, however, two prefatory remarks. First, I want to declare an interest. As the coeditor of *Why Some People Are Healthy and Others Not: The Determinants of Population Health*, I found the public health sections of this paper annoyingly self-referential: the main empirical research they cite is their own. Although I am not an epidemiologist, I spent five years meeting regularly with a number of Canadian social scientists who wrote the basic chapters of that book. Nothing in this article makes a large advance over the understanding that book communicated nearly six years ago. What's more, there is considerable evidence that Kennedy and Kawachi did not carefully consider its findings. More generally, the authors' whole discussion seems curiously disconnected from the extensive research that precedes their work. *The Lalonde Report* of 1975, the most widely distributed public document in Canadian history, argued that, at the levels of income in societies like Canada's, conventional investments in medical care were unlikely to produce big improvements in population health. Not a word about that, let alone about the efforts of scholars like James House of the University of Michigan to chart the causal pathways by which "social determinants" work their health effects, appears in their essay. And there is only a throwaway line about what may be the most illuminating research on these questions—the Whitehall study that Michael Marmot has pioneered. In that study, the gradient in health outcomes, given equal exposure to risk, appeared to be connected to the amount of control over their lives that differently situated workers have. Daniels, Kennedy, and Kawachi say little about the physical pathways that might account for these differences—even though Marmot, and others, have explored them.

Second, space considerations prevent my taking up the theoretical issues raised by the authors' treatment of how justice claims and the social determinants of health are linked. This is a serious topic, done with considerable care in the article, and worthy of separate analysis. Instead, I want to focus on a couple of key points.

How Bad Is Inequality?

Have the authors made a compelling case for the claim that "justice is good for our health"? I think not, but one needs to begin by asking what precisely the authors are asserting. The most cautious presumption is that inequality appears to affect the health of populations. That, of course, is consistent with the correlations the authors present. But there is little in the way of a rigorous defense of this claim. One difficulty is that the precise meaning they attach to "inequality" is unclear: sometimes it seems to mean the Gini coefficient (a standard measure of income dispersion), and sometimes (as with the section on the Rawlsian conception of justice) it seems to be linked to the distribution of stress and control at work.

But the most important problems, I suspect, are the technical arguments against using correlations—whether at the national, state, or local level—to support causal claims. Scholars such as Harold Pollack of Michigan, Jeff Milyo of Tufts, and Ingrid Ellen of New York University all contest the idea that, controlling for income, inequality itself necessarily matters. As Pollack put it recently at an academic meeting, "cross-sectional regressions that use inequality measures such as Gini are virtually uninterpretable." He goes on to say that "it is frustrating that uncritical use of these measures is so pervasive in public health analyses of [United States] and cross-national comparisons." Pollack's grounds, which I find plausible, are straightforward: "Money matters near the bottom of the distribution and may not matter at all for many outcomes when one exceeds the median. Controlling for the median income, then, any income dispersion measure is highly correlated with the percentage of the population under the poverty line."[1] So it is not dispersion itself that matters for health, but the proportion of the population that is poor.

The connection between inequality and health, then, is far from obvious to other analysts and this article does little to dispel the skepticism Pollack's remarks exhibit. That does not mean there are no connections between inequality and health. Rather, the connections are less obvious than the article suggests, and their implications, for what counts as a just society or what policies such societies should pursue, are less compelling than presented.

POLICY IMPLICATIONS?

I turn now to the topic with which I am most familiar: drawing policy implications from admittedly controversial empirical findings. Assume for the moment that the article's central contention about inequality and health is correct. Assume further that we know how to reduce income inequalities, that the technology of redistribution is available and implementable. Does that mean we should turn to inequality-reducing policies as a matter of health policy, subordinating the claims on resources made by modern medicine?

The authors' discussion of this issue is more nuanced than their treatment of the social determinants of health. Daniels, Kennedy, and Kawachi concede that identifiable illness commands our attention and utilitarian concerns about "net benefits" need not always trump our humane allocation of care for the ill. But two larger issues of public policy analysis remain. First, the discussion of the purposes of health care policy is terribly truncated. National health insurance finds justification not simply in efforts to improve on measures of a population's health. We care about equality of access to medical care because suffering, pain, uncertainty, and the myriad other features of being ill or injured ought not, it is widely believed, vary primarily with one's ability to pay. The fact that even in systems of universal health insurance there are pockets of unequal response to illness does not dispel the egalitarian aspiration—or the social cohesion and sense of fairness—that such efforts both reflect and symbolize.

Second, I am concerned that the authors understate the gains that fairness in allocating medical care has proved capable of generating, and that they overstate the likelihood that we can do very much about more basic determinants of social equality.

Put more generally, there is no reason to treat a theoretical possibility as a compelling policy option unless both the worth of that aim and its implementability dominate the alternatives. Nothing in contemporary America suggests that we are likely to move more quickly in reducing income inequality than we are to make health care more fairly available. The expected value of a policy option is, in short, its idealized results times the likelihood of achieving them. A one-in-ten chance of getting a dollar is a lot less valuable, looked at this way, than a one-in-two chance of getting fifty cents; indeed the latter is two-and-a-half times better.

It is worth remembering that when national health insurance was a more prominent option in the 1970s one of the arguments against it was that medical care outlays were wasted, that more powerful tools for improving America's health were available. A quarter of a century later, Americans enjoy longer life spans, but with a distribution of health care that is shameful. Those nations with a reasonably fair distribution of income protection against the costs of illness might well gain by concentrating at the margin on health-improving policies outside of medical care. The United States, I contend, should address the doable but difficult task of making medical care more fairly distributed before taking on the more utopian task that Daniels and colleagues suggest.

POLITICAL PROBLEMS

EZEKIEL EMANUEL

That social factors strongly influence health and life expectancy is well established news. Indeed, the classic finding in this regard is that life expectancy in the United States and Britain, for instance, rose dramatically at the end of the nineteenth century. This is generally attributed to social factors—better housing, water treatment, working conditions, and nutrition—because effective medical interventions came much later (surgery did not become safe until the turn of the century, penicillin was not manufactured in large quantities until World War II, chronic dialysis did not become available until the early 1960s, resuscitation was first reported in 1960, and the intensive care unit did not become a fixture in hospitals until the late 1960s). Reinforcing this link between social factors and health outcomes are numerous studies both in the United States and abroad of the causes for the substantial and persistent decline in cardiovascular mortality since the 1960s. They show that about half of the decline is due to "social factors," such as smoking cessation and changes in diet, while 40 percent or so of the decline is attributable to direct medical interventions, such as better control of blood pressure, cardiac surgery, and cardiac care units.

The real issue is what to do about this information. How should the understanding that social factors have a profound and significant impact on health outcomes and inequalities affect research and social policies? Daniels, Kennedy, and Kawachi suggest that we should stop concentrating on health care and look "upstream." Our attention should be focused on access to basic education, level of material deprivation, quality of workplace environment, and equality of political participation. While Daniels and colleagues (strangely) single out bioethicists for chastisement, their admonition to stop worrying about exotic new technologies, the doctor-patient relationship, the performance of managed care, and even the fair allocation of health care resources seems directed to everyone—health policy experts, health care administrators, politicians, and the general public. Their advice: if you care about improving the health of the country, stop obsessing about "increasing access to medical care" and campaign for social justice. This is what Michael Marmot and others once called "the extreme version of the upstream focus [in which] action to reduce inequalities in health should therefore focus on the causes of social inequalities." It is strange to hear this call at the very moment expanding access to medical care has again surfaced in national debate for the first time since the 1993 Clinton debacle.

Who could disagree that we should focus more attention on social justice? Even if they had absolutely no impact on health, narrowing income inequality in the United States, improving the educational system, and reforming the political process to reduce the influence of money and enhance popular participation are independently worthy goals that demand our attention. However, linking them to health outcomes—making improving health an important reason and motivation to advocate social justice—will likely be ineffectual. It may well be counterproductive, at least in the United States.

First, it is highly unlikely that Americans are going to be roused to support improvements in social justice because such changes will (or, more accurately, may) lead to improvements in health outcomes. Those of us dedicated to a more just society find the American public's toleration of gross—and growing—inequalities in income and political power puzzling and frustrating. Yet this is the reality in which changes will have to be fashioned. While Americans do not seem interested in lower taxes at the moment, neither are they clamoring for higher marginal tax rates on the rich; while they want campaign finance reform, it is hardly a burning issue that will determine more than a handful of votes. The one issue of social justice that inflames Americans is education. And this is because it will lead not to better health outcomes but to economic advancement; people worry that the educational system is failing many kids, including their own, and is thereby locking them out of good jobs in the future.

As politically salient as health care is, it hardly seems as if the American public, at least, is likely to be persuaded to support higher marginal tax rates, campaign finance reform, or a host of other things because these changes may narrow health inequalities or even improve their own health. Somehow "Support higher taxes on the rich and live longer" or "Ban soft money and improve your health" are unlikely to be persuasive or plausible to the public.

If we want to reduce health inequalities and to improve health outcomes, following Daniels and colleagues by focusing "upstream" and getting bioethicists, health policy experts, and the public discussion to focus on income inequality is likely to be even more frustrating than focusing directly on health care has been for the last thirty years. And this is probably not limited to the United States. Aversion to wealth redistribution and income equality may be more extreme in the United States than elsewhere, but throughout the developed world the embrace is of more, rather than less, socioeconomic inequality. Health care is unlikely to be the horse to carry social justice measures over the finish line.

Linking health improvement too closely to social justice could actually backfire. In the United States, health care programs have won broad support for many years. This is true not only for funding of the National Institutes of Health but also for support of Medicare and other health programs, in part because health care is viewed as something that benefits everyone in society. Health programs are not viewed as special-interest programs or as programs for the poor, racial minorities, or other groups. As Rashi Fein has pointed out, the difference in support of Medicaid and Medicare is closely linked to one being viewed as a "poor person's" program and the other a general program that also happens to benefit the poor. Whether we like it or not, it is precisely because health care is viewed as key to equal opportunity, without overtly or intentionally redistributing income, that it garners such strong public support. This is an essential foundation piece for any chance of forging a majority to support some version of universal health coverage in the United States.

Convincing the American public to look "upstream" and make general redistributive efforts key to improving health is unlikely to promote redistribution and could well undermine health care; resistance to redistribution is likely to be stronger than endorsement of expanded access to health care. Indeed, the more Americans are told how much redistribution Daniels, Kennedy, and Kawachi contemplate to secure health improvements—income inequalities less "than those observed in even the most industrialized countries," early childhood interventions that "go beyond the best models of such interventions we see in European efforts," and so on—the more dismissive they are likely to be of gazing "upstream."

Finally, there is another reason why focusing "upstream" may actually be counterproductive to improving health: the voracious consumption of resources by health care threatens to preclude investment in all other social services including the very education and income transfer programs Daniels and colleagues argue are necessary to remove health disparities. In the early 1990s, health care was consuming so much of state budgets that it eroded funding for any other valuable social programs; Medicaid costs were eating up dollars for education, the environment, the arts, and everything else. A combination of managed care, which held down costs, albeit in a one-time manner, and the booming economy saved state budgets from the Medicaid juggernaut. Today, state coffers are overflowing and health care costs are hardly a concern to state legislatures. But this cannot last forever. The days of low health care inflation are over. Rising costs will begin to drive up Medicaid budgets. Furthermore the business expansion—and seemingly unlimited tax proceeds it has produced—will have to end. The inevitable recession will cut state revenues just at the time that health care costs will rise. Consequently, all non–health care spending will be threatened. Unless there is attention to prudent allocation of health care services and coverage, the very social programs Daniels, Kennedy, and Kawachi deem essential to eliminating health inequities—education, day care, income transfers, environmental improvements, etc.—will be imperiled by health care costs. And much the same can be said for Medicare at the federal level. So the paradox is, excessive health care costs are the direct threat to the reforms Daniels and colleagues want to improve health. Focusing upstream will prevent the focus necessary to ensure governmental budgets have sufficient resources to attend to something other than health care. In this way the Daniels/Kennedy/ Kawachi prescription may be very dangerous.

So what should be done about these data? One objective is to determine the effect of narrowing income inequality on the health of the "best off." While it is strange to worry about the best off, if narrowing income inequality improves overall health by raising the low end but somehow decreases the health of the rich, they are likely to resist. There is no reason to think this will occur. Indeed, Medicare shows the opposite; it produced general improvements in health delivery that benefited the well off. But demonstrating a "trickle up" for the health of the well off would undercut at least this element of opposition to social justice.

Another lesson is to design health interventions that take into account the differential impact on lower socioeconomic groups. Smoking cessation targeted at minorities, universal prenatal care that ensures coverage for the poor, and opposing development and coverage of services that only the rich will have access to all utilize the knowledge gained while sustaining support for health.

Finally, bioethicists, health policy experts, and others should keep the focus on universal access and the just allocation of health care resources. Most Americans are dissatisfied with the current health care system; what is needed is an alternative a majority can endorse. While this may not have the same total impact on improving health outcomes as substantial income redistribution, health care services still account for 25 to 40 percent of improvements in health outcomes. This is substantial, worth securing for everyone, and will enhance social justice. And it is part of the current public discussion.

Admonishing caution in shifting the perspective of bioethicists, health policy experts, and the public "upstream" should be construed as neither an argument against greater efforts at social justice nor a dismissal of the importance of the social determinants of health, but as a warning not to forsake attention to greater access to health care.

PRIMARY CARE

BARBARA STARFIELD

No one who is concerned with justice as a basic principle would deny the value of income redistribution, particularly in view of the powerful relationship between income inequality and ill health. The policy question turns on issues of feasibility, practicality, and time frame. What might be complementary strategies while the struggle for income redistribution takes place?

Most people know that the United States has the most costly health system in the world, but few realize that the health of the U.S. population is worse than that of the populations of many other industrialized nations. The only major health indicator for which the United States is *not* near the bottom of the rankings is life expectancy at age 80 or older. In the general scheme of things, there are many determinants of ill health (biological, social, psychological, environmental, genetic), and they are likely to act in ways that differ in different population subgroups. While more doctors, more hospitals, and more technology rarely, if ever, produce better health of populations, certain aspects of health systems do have a positive impact on health. That is, relatively new health policy studies show that health systems achieve better health if they are better oriented to primary care, with specialty care serving primary care rather than the other way around. As a strategy for achieving equity in health services delivery, primary care is generally associated with other progressive political approaches, such as more equitable tax policies and better distribution of income. But even then, studies have shown that areas that are better endowed with primary care physicians and less well endowed with specialists have better health as measured by a wide variety of health indicators, regardless of the degree of income inequality. This is the case both internationally and within all fifty U.S. states. Still, the strength of the relationship between primary care resources and health varies across different population subgroups, indicating that other determinants also play an important role.

Most people in the United States think that having free access to specialists assures them the best quality of care, thus reflecting an unmitigated faith in the power of medical and surgical tests and procedures. Although access to specialists is important for those who need it, unrestrained access to specialists is potentially dangerous. Unnecessary technology, which is more often applied by specialists than by primary care physicians, can be harmful to health. The same is true of many medications. The unanticipated adverse effects of technology and medications, along with the adverse effects due to errors in their administration, account for somewhere between the third and fourth leading cause of death in the United States.

A long-term relationship with a primary care practitioner can help people decide when specialty care is not really needed, thus reducing the ill effects of nonindicated interventions. Public awareness of the importance of improving primary care, including appropriate referral to specialists when indicated, is critical to improving the health of the population. It is no accident that the elderly have the best health status (relative to other countries): they are the only segment of the population with continuous assured financial access to health services since 1965, which made it possible to build long-term relationships with primary care physicians.

Income redistribution may go a long way toward improving health, but there will also have to be simultaneous attention to changing other social and health policies. As one pundit said, "For every complex problem, there is a simple solution, and it is wrong." There is no simple solution to reducing systematic health inequalities. A policy reorientation that recognizes the importance of universal access to high-quality primary care services backed up, when indicated, by appropriate specialty care resources, is a critical part of the strategy. Managed care has derailed a national focus on building a strong primary care infrastructure by pretending to be organized around primary care. In its focus on profit making and cost cutting, managed care, in its current incarnation, fails to fulfill any of the important functions of good primary care.

Unfortunately, a poorly informed public focuses on the ills of managed care without understanding how managed care got here in the first place. People want direct access to specialists, in the mistaken belief that this will improve their health, without any recognition that they risk harm to health from overuse of potentially dangerous interventions. The evidence is clear that the best way to achieve better health is to greatly enhance the contributions of primary care, which focuses on meeting and solving people's health needs, including appropriate referrals when they are indicated. A more informed public and better public policy will have to be marshaled to address the many possible approaches to reducing the systematic disparities in health across population subgroups and the relatively dismal health status of this nation. Income redistribution is important, but it is unlikely to happen any time soon. In the meantime, other strategies, including improving the equity-enhancing aspects of health systems, are likely to be more practical and feasible.

A HEALTH AGENDA

EMMANUELA GAKIDOU, JULIO FRENK,
AND CHRISTOPHER MURRAY

The paper by Daniels, Kennedy, and Kawachi is an important piece from the perspectives of social epidemiology, ethics, and policy. It raises critical issues about the determinants of health inequalities and proposes policies that might contribute to their reduction.

We at the World Health Organization (WHO) give great importance to the reduction of health inequality. In a new framework for the assessment of health system performance proposed by the WHO, reducing health inequality is one of four main goals for health systems. The other three goals are improving health status, enhancing the responsiveness of the health system to the legitimate expectations of the population, and protecting people in a fair manner from the financial consequences of caring for health. By explicitly listing the reduction of health inequality as one of the intrinsic goals of health systems, the WHO illustrates the prominence that this problem should receive in the health policy agenda.

Daniels, Kennedy, and Kawachi make four policy recommendations for the reduction of health inequalities—all of which constitute social policies that do not primarily involve the health sector. They suggest that "to address comprehensively the problem of health inequalities, governments must begin to address the issue of economic inequalities." We agree that economic redistribution policies are intrinsically important, independent of their effect on the reduction of health inequalities, and as such should constitute good social policies regardless of the degree of health inequalities present in a society. Similarly, we consider health to be intrinsically important, independent of its association with other components of well-being.

When it comes to health, specialized entities, both at the international level (e.g., the WHO) and the national level (e.g., various ministries of health), have great potential to influence policies aimed at the reduction of health inequalities. They also have the capacity to be involved in intersectoral approaches aimed at improving specific determinants of health. But these entities can only do so much. For example, it may be possible to convince ministries of finance to raise taxes on tobacco, yet ministries of health typically have little capacity to influence broad economic redistribution policies. Therefore, these actors typically concentrate on within-the-health-sector approaches and on intersectoral initiatives to improve specific determinants of health.

Before making explicit policy recommendations we need to be better informed about how health systems of various countries perform in the achievement of their goals. Once we have a better understanding of the factors influencing the performance of a health system we will be better equipped to articulate policies that will lead to the reduction of inequalities.

Health Inequality

We define health inequality to be the differences in health across individuals in a population. We are using the individual as the unit of analysis and are interested in studying the inequality in the distribution of health. We propose to use health expectancy as the measure of health. Health expectancy—the number of years that an individual born today is expected to live in the equivalent of full health—reflects the risk of mortality and the risk of nonfatal health outcomes that an individual faces at each age. It is important that the measure of health reflects not only the risk of death but also the risk of being in ill health.

Before we try to measure inequality of health expectancy, though, we first ask what, if any, components of health expectancy either are not amenable to change or arise from fully informed choices of individuals to decrease their health expectancy through the pursuit of risky activities. If there are differences that could never be remedied by intervention or new technology, one might argue that we should be uninterested in them. But what component of the distribution of health expectancy is not amenable to intervention? That due to genes? That due to chance during birth? In both cases, the argument that we cannot intervene to change the effects on the distribution of health expectancy seems specious. There is little evidence of significant cross-population variation in the contribution of genes. And with current improvements in technology and future progress, it is likely that even genes will become amenable to change.

What about volition? How much of the distribution of health expectancy for a population is due to fully informed choices of individuals who have a taste for risky behavior? This seems like a very slippery slope. What choices affecting health are fully informed? Would we exclude the effects of tobacco on health expectancy because smoking is a choice? Even if we claim that the choice was informed, should it be excluded? We argue that it should not be excluded. First, in most cases health risks are adopted not because of a love of risky behavior but rather for other, less informed reasons.[1] Second, the true volitional component of the distribution of health expectancy is likely to be very small and can well be ignored. This argument is similar to ones used to explain certain measures of income inequality, where the variation in the distribution of income due to different trade-offs between leisure and income within the population is routinely ignored in the measurement of income inequality.

Finally we ask, how can health expectancy be measured? Risk, after all, is not observed; only outcomes are. But the distribution of health risks can be reasonably approximated through a variety of techniques. Together, they allow us to measure the distribution of four key dimensions: child mortality risk, adult mortality risk, life expectancy and health expectancy through small-area analyses, and nonfatal health outcomes.

1. Child Mortality Risk. We can observe the variation in the proportion of a mother's children who have died, which provides information at a very fine level of aggregation (namely households) on the distribution of child death risk. Using simulation, we can evaluate the difference in the distribution of outcomes from that which would be expected based on a distribution of equal risk. Data on children ever born and children surviving for women of different ages are widely available from the Living Standards Measurement Studies (LSMS), the Demographic and Health Surveys (DHS), and many censuses and surveys. We have implemented this strategy for measuring child mortality.

2. Adult Mortality Risk. We do not have good data to measure the distribution of adult mortality. Information on the survivorship of siblings could in principle be used, but it would refer to average mortality experience over decades and the technical challenges have yet to be solved. Other strategies need to be developed.

3. Life Expectancy or Health Expectancy for Groups. We can divide the population into groups that are expected to have similar health expectancies and measure directly the health expectation for those groups. Inevitably, this will underestimate the distribution of health expectancy. The more refined the groupings are, the more we will approximate the true underlying distribution. Small-area analyses hold out the promise of being one of the most refined methods for revealing the underlying distribution of health expectancy in a population. For example, a detailed age-sex-race group analysis of counties in the United States has revealed a range in life expectancy across counties of 41.3 years—almost as large as the range across all countries of the world.

4. Nonfatal Health Outcomes. Measurement of nonfatal health outcomes on continuous or polychotomous scales provides more information from which to estimate the distribution of risk across individuals. Numerous surveys provide information on self-reported health status using a variety of instruments. The main problem to date with this information is the comparability of the responses across different cultures, levels of educational attainment, and incomes. For example, the rich often report worse nonfatal health outcomes than the poor. Problems of comparability must be resolved before such data sets can be used to contribute to estimation of health expectancy in the population.

For the WHO, the way forward will be to simultaneously pursue the development of methods and data sets to measure these different dimensions of the distribution of health expectancy. We recognize that there is a great need for new methods to integrate these different measurements into one estimation of the distribution of health expectancy in populations. Based on the wide array of measures used to summarize the distribution of income several measures of the distribution of health expectancy can be developed.

Determinants of Health Inequality

The measurement of health inequalities across countries is a crucial step toward a better understanding of its determinants. Once the performance of the health system has been assessed with respect to each goal, including the reduction of health inequalities, we intend to proceed with analytical work on the determinants of performance.

The study of the determinants of health and its distribution will involve those socioeconomic variables that are likely to play an important role. The relationship between socioeconomic status and health is complex, and we would like to differentiate among the following four interactions, each of which is very important and needs to be better understood: (1) how the average level of socioeconomic status affects the average level of health in a population; (2) how the average level of socioeconomic status influences the distribution of health; (3) how the distribution of socioeconomic status affects the average health; and (4) how the distribution of socioeconomic status influences the distribution of health in a population.

The framework presented above will provide us with the opportunity to study these relationships, since individuals have been used as the unit of analysis in the measurement of health and health inequality. Individual-level data provide us with a greater capacity to analyze this complex relationship than do aggregate-level data. This approach has been criticized by those looking at differences in health status across social groups for ignoring the important relationship between socioeconomic status and health. On the contrary, our proposed measurement strategy will use socioeconomic status and its distribution as potential determinants of health inequality. When individuals are grouped by a socioeconomic variable and differences in health status across these groups are reported, the *a priori* assumption is made that the variable used to group individuals is the most important determinant of health inequality. Our approach does not make any *a priori* assumptions in the measurement of health inequality but uses potential determinants, including socioeconomic status, as explanatory variables. Both approaches, however, recognize that socioeconomic status and its distribution may be powerful determinants of health inequality.

The reduction of health inequalities is a key goal of health systems. Once the complex web of determination of these inequalities is better understood, there will be a pressing need for policies aimed at reducing them. The health system will play a central role in the formulation and implementation of these policies, whereby efforts directed specifically at health care institutions will have to be accompanied by initiatives involving other sectors.

LOST IN TRANSLATION

STEFFIE WOOLHANDLER AND
DAVID HIMMELSTEIN

In the 1920s, a major current of Soviet health planning con-
templated the withering away of curative medicine. Many
believed that as socialism evolved into communism—eliminating inequality, poverty, alienation, and oppression—
prevention, in the broadest sense, would obviate the need for
doctors and hospitals.

This Soviet view was an extreme, caricatured version of a
long, more holistic socialist tradition. Rudolf Virchow (the
founder of modern pathology) and Friedrich Engels ana-
lyzed the social determinants of disease in Silesia and the
British working class, respectively. Early in his career, Sal-
vador Allende (then minister of health in a Popular Front
government) described the social origin of disease and
suffering in his book *La Realidad Medico-Social Chilena* and
concluded that only broad structural change in Chilean society could adequately address health problems.

The Marxist tradition has delineated a socialized biology: patterns of health, disease, and even physiology that
are shaped in interaction with a specific social environment. As Richard Levins has pointed out, there is a "late-
twentieth-century capitalist" pancreas, not in the sense of a

particularly wealthy organ, but rather an organ stressed to the point of diabetes by a variety of socially determined factors: patterns of diet dictated by agribusiness, living and school environments antagonistic to exercise, work situations that constrain meal schedules and physical activity, and a profit-driven health care system that fails to embrace prevention.

Recent work on inequalities in health, which forms the empirical foundation for Daniels, Kennedy, and Kawachi's piece, is a statistical restatement and verification of this tradition: Virchow's and Engels's prose descriptions are being translated into the modern scientific language of epidemiology. Such translation is a great service; it presents alien and suspect ideas in acceptable academic format. Concern over social and health inequality has become a legitimate focus for academic work, encouraging altruism among colleagues and students, and providing ammunition for progressive reformers. Press attention has followed, and with it, pressure on policy makers to ameliorate inequality.

But in the translation from socialism to epidemiology something has also been lost. In analyzing typhus, Virchow found the social seeds of disease and prescribed (and participated in) efforts to overthrow a social system in which "thousands always must die in misery so that a few hundred may live well." Allende's prescription for the ill health due to social inequality was a united front to uproot capitalism and imperialism in Chile.

Daniels, Kennedy, and Kawachi describe the phenomenology of inequality and injustice but leave its origins and perpetrators obscured. Hence their prescriptions call for a change in policy, but not in power. They would redistribute wealth but don't renounce the reign of the market or the inviolability of property rights that are the mother and father of inequality.

Failing to identify the perpetrators of poverty and inequality can also lead to confusion over policy choices. Daniels, Kennedy, and Kawachi imply that resources might profitably be shifted from a profligate health care system into programs to upgrade the standard of living for the poor. In Canada, the health minister published a more explicit statement of a similar view. Yet when health care was cut, the resources were transferred to the rich, not to the poor.

The people and institutions (the corporate elite or ruling class) that benefit from the unequal provision of health care also benefit from the unequal distribution of wealth, education, and power. When these powerful groups are weakened, through popular mobilization, inequality shrinks and health care improves. Thus, the Great Society social programs of the 1960s substantially shrank inequalities in income, education, wealth, and housing—and coincided with the passage of Medicare and Medicaid. In Sweden, recent cuts in health spending have coincided with a more general attack on the welfare state.

Finally, we would raise three minor quibbles with Daniels, Kennedy, and Kawachi. First, health care is so expensive in the United States that for sick people inadequate insurance often means poverty. Indeed, ill health is the leading cause of personal bankruptcy. Second, we are uncomfortable with their implication that health is the key metric for measuring a society. Does Japanese longevity make Japan a model society? Third, analyses focused on inequality should not obscure the horrific absolute deprivation in our society. In 1995, 11.6 million Americans went hungry, 4.4 million had their gas or electricity turned off, and 1 million were evicted from their homes.

These criticisms should not detract from the great service that Daniels, Kennedy, and Kawachi have performed in this paper and elsewhere. They have been effective leaders in academia in the fight for equality and justice.

3

REPLY

NORMAN DANIELS, BRUCE KENNEDY,
AND ICHIRO KAWACHI

Justice is good for our health in two ways. At the "point of delivery," justice requires universal access to a system of health care that meets our health needs fairly under resource constraints. "Upstream" from the health care system, justice demands fair distributions of liberty, opportunity, and basic resources. Achieving these fair distributions—correctly specified, we think, by John Rawls's theory of justice—turns out to be a crucial determinant of public health, so that justice improves overall population health while reducing health inequalities. Our policies must keep both pursuits of justice in view. Justice in the delivery of health care and background justice in the society are both good for our health.

With that brief summary of our view, we turn to the comments by respondents on our empirical, philosophical, and policy claims.

Empirics

The empirical section of our essay presented some basic ideas about the social determinants of health for a general

{ 85 }

reader; we did not offer, as Marmor rightly says, a comprehensive discussion, let alone historical review, for an expert audience. Our brevity, however, may have produced some misunderstandings that we would like now to address.

Several respondents suggest that much health inequality can be attributed to the difference between the very poor and everyone else, rather than to inequalities in the population as a whole. If their claim is right, then public policy ought to focus on getting the very poor above an acceptable threshold but should worry less about inequalities in the rest of the population.

We are doubtful about the underlying claim. Recall that one of the most intriguing findings we reported is the socioeconomic gradient in health status: though the poorest individuals are at the greatest risk of dying compared to the richest, the excess risk for mortality does not stop there. Even individuals with household incomes in the $50,000 to $70,000 range experience excess risk of death compared to the most affluent group. This difference in risk of death cannot be due to the former being unable to afford the basic necessities of life; some other processes are at work. Moreover, this finding holds across countries and within relatively middle-income groups. We mentioned, for example, the Whitehall study of British civil servants. The participants in this study might all be classified as white-collar workers with steady employment and access to universal health care; they were certainly not in poverty. Yet even in this reasonably well off cohort, the lowest occupation grades have four times the mortality risks of the top grade. Health inequalities are not simply a matter of the poor versus everyone else.

In a similar vein, Ted Marmor and Marcia Angell suggest that the relationship between income inequality and health in the United States might be attributable simply to differences in pockets of poverty across states, so that the states with more or larger pockets of poverty would also have worse average health outcomes. Several recent studies have addressed this possibility by including individual income and health outcomes along with state-level measures of income distribution. These studies show that even when we control for individual income, thereby accounting for between-state differences in the number of poor individuals, individuals living in states with high levels of income inequality have poorer health outcomes than those living in more egalitarian states, regardless of their own individual income. To be sure, individuals with the lowest incomes are worst off in health terms as well. But even those with middle incomes have worse health outcomes than their counterparts in states with more equitable income distributions. These studies show that the observed relationship between income inequality and health is not simply a function of the underlying association between individual income itself and health. Of course, being well off is good for your health. But living in a more equal society is also good for your health.

Moreover, and finally, income inequality is not a "mysterious" cause of undesirable health outcomes. It works through identifiable causal pathways, including unequal access to opportunities such as education, healthy employment, and health care; reduced social cohesion; distortions in political participation; and the stress effects of relative lack of control. These pathways are in and of themselves important contributors to health and well-being and should serve as relatively uncontroversial levers for policy intervention.

PHILOSOPHY

Social justice is an important value, independent of its impact on health. Ezekiel Emanuel and other respondents emphasize this point, and we entirely agree. We don't just want justice exclusively because it promotes population health or a fair distribution of health care.

Nevertheless, health is such a basic good that any plausible account of justice must say something about the distribution of health care in a society. Amartya Sen's theory, as Marmot notes, goes directly to the issue. According to Sen, the point of justice is to promote our "positive freedom," our ability to be and do what we choose. Disease and disability strike at the heart of that ability: they directly diminish our capability to function well. And because they do, justice directly requires an appropriate distribution of the social determinants of health.

On John Rawls's theory of justice, things are more complicated. Justice, according to Rawls, requires a fair distribution of basic liberties, opportunities, and economic resources: health does not figure directly in the view. Still, two lines of argument connect Rawlsian ideas of justice to concerns about health care. The first argument rests on the empirical discovery, described in our article, that achieving a fair distribution of liberties, opportunity, and economic resources *also* causes a fair distribution of population health. As Anand and Peter suggest, there might have been no such relationship between the principles of justice and a fair distribution of public heath. The principles might not have addressed the key social determinants of health at all, or they might have resulted in greater health inequality. The second argument involves an extension of Rawls's theory that does make the reduction of health inequalities a direct requirement of justice. The idea is that we cannot ensure to people the reasonable array of opportunities that justice requires without protecting healthy functioning: serious impairments of health mean serious limits on opportunities. Because justice requires such a reasonable array, we must ensure a proper distribution of the social determinants of health, once we discover what they are.

Anand and Peter find a "tension" between these two arguments: while we argue here that Rawlsian principles indirectly and fortuitously assure an equitable distribution of health, the extension of Rawls's view proposed by Daniels directly requires equitable distribution because it includes an assurance of normal functioning in the guarantee of equal opportunity. So it may seem "redundant" to appeal to other principles as a way of securing the equitable distribution of health. In particular, it may seem redundant to emphasize the importance of fair income distribution for public health. Opportunity does it all.

We find neither "tension" nor "redundancy," but a happy convergence of two lines of argument. We do not intend to propose two theories of justice bearing on health but only one, the extended theory that addresses health through its effects on opportunity. When we discover what the key social determinants of health are, we conclude—via the equal opportunity principle—that justice requires these determinants to be distributed in whatever ways produce equity in the distribution of health. At the same time, we observe that the other principles of justice support a similar conclusion. So the theory produces a convergence, not tension or redundancy. Had the facts about the social determinants been different—for example, had greater income equality been detrimental to public health—we might have had a much more troubling result, inasmuch as different principles of justice, with independent value, might then have worked at cross-purposes.

A final point on philosophy: Unlike Marmot, we see a convergence of Sen's and Rawls's views, at least once the extension of Rawls's theory to health is made. In his early work, Sen argued that Rawls's emphasis on liberties, opportunity, and economic resources obscured the problems produced by disease and disability. Consider two people with exactly the same liberties, opportunities, and economic resources but one of whom is disabled: these two would have very different levels of positive freedom—different "capabilities for functioning," as Sen puts it—but Rawls's theory would, he said, obscure this difference. So Sen urged that our views about justice should focus directly on our real capabilities for doing things, and not simply on our liberties, opportunities, and economic resources.

Once it is understood, however, that assurances of normal functioning are included in the idea of a reasonable array of opportunities, Rawls has a way to blunt the force of Sen's criticism: he can register the difference that a disability makes precisely as a difference in opportunity. From Sen's side, his *Development as Freedom* focuses on the protections of liberties and opportunities in ways that make him address issues long of central concern to Rawls. Terminology aside, there is less difference than meets the eye.

POLICY

A final set of comments relates to the role of health care in reducing health inequalities. Marmor and Emanuel take issue with our emphasis on reducing social disparities and suggest that the more urgent public policy problem is lack of access to health care in this country. There is, of course, no gainsaying that medical care contributes to the health of individuals and populations. And as Barbara Starfield notes, primary care is particularly effective and important.

It should not be overlooked in discussions of how society should go about reducing health inequalities.

Nonetheless, we disagree with Marmor's false forced choice analogy—that we must somehow *choose* between expanding coverage of health care and devoting our energies to changing the social distribution of other resources (income, education, and opportunities for healthy work). These are not competing objectives but synergistic goals. Popular support for universal health care coverage *arises* (when it does) out of a shared egalitarian ethos that is itself a product of maintaining a relatively short distance between the top and bottom of the social hierarchy. Witness, for example, the birth of the National Health Service, which arose in Britain during an unusually cohesive, egalitarian environment that followed the Second World War. Conversely, societies that tolerate a high degree of inequality, such as the United States, also have enormous difficulty in forging a consensus about providing such communal benefits as health care. When the social distance between the "haves" and "have nots" is wide, there is correspondingly little motivation for those who are already covered by health insurance to care about the plight of the uninsured.

A broader social movement seeking a more egalitarian distribution of resources may well be a precondition for conducting a meaningful national debate about universal health care (and for addressing the issues of power that Woolhandler and Himmelstein raise). It is probably no accident that the failed reform efforts of the Clinton administration appealed to middle-class self-interest and to the self-interest of large employers worried about costs, with no appeal to the moral considerations about equality and fairness that lie at the heart of universal coverage. To concentrate our efforts on expanding health care coverage just because it seems more "doable" is therefore to confuse the prescription with the cause of the underlying illness.

Marmor's excellent book *Why Some People Are Healthy and Others Not* rendered a valuable service by reminding us that access to health care is not the major determinant of health inequalities. Again, the experience of the National Health Service in Britain has taught us that provision of universal health care does not by itself eliminate or reduce health disparities (in fact, they have widened). The Whitehall studies similarly indicate that among individuals who have access to the same health care service there can be three- to fourfold differences in the risk of premature mortality according to one's access to other resources (the amount of control on the job, prestige, income and wealth, and so on). In other words, a society interested in reducing health inequalities is unlikely to do so by focusing on the provision of health care alone. Policies to improve population health must concern themselves as much with the *sources* of health (and correcting inequalities in their distribution) as with the instrumental means of curing illnesses (i.e., the provision of health care).

We would agree with the view that adding poor health to the list of outcomes associated with income maldistribution is unlikely to spark a revolution, or to make Americans care more about trends in income distribution. The point we wish to reiterate is that good health (which most people *do* care about) depends to a large extent on factors that lie outside the health care sector, and that a society wishing to reduce health inequalities needs to engage willingly in intersectoral efforts—early childhood investment, narrowing the income gap, ensuring healthy workplaces, and other similar policies mentioned in our essay.

Health is too important to be left to the doctors alone.

NOTES

AMARTYA SEN / *Foreword*

1. See James Boswell, *The Life of Samuel Johnson* (London: J. M. Dent, and New York: E. P. Dent, 1925), volume II, p. 240.

2. Ibid.

3. On this see James E. Meade, *The Just Economy* (London: Macmillan, 1976); A. B. Atkinson, *Social Justice and Public Policy* (Brighton: Wheatsheaf, and Cambridge: MIT Press, 1983).

4. I have discussed this question in "Equality of What?" in S. McMurrin, ed., *Tanner Lectures on Human Values*, vol. I (Cambridge, England: Cambridge University Press, and Salt Lake City: University of Utah Press, 1980), and *Inequality Reexamined* (Oxford: Clarendon Press, and Cambridge: Harvard University Press, 1992).

5. See John Rawls, *A Theory of Justice* (Cambridge: Harvard University Press, 1971), and *Political Liberalism* (New York: Columbia University Press, 1993).

6. The distinctions are extensively discussed in the Ph.D. dissertation of Jennifer Prah Ruger, "Aristotelian Justice and Health Policy: Capability and Incompletely Theorized Agreements" (Harvard University, 1998).

7. See Norman Daniels, *Justice and Justification: Reflective Equilibrium in Theory and Practice* (Cambridge, England: Cambridge University Press, 1996).

8. See also Douglas Black et al., *Inequalities in Health: The Black Report, The Health Divide* (London: Penguin, 1988). On the extensive pattern of inter-country differentials, see also Richard G. Wilkinson, *Unhealthy Societies* (London: Routledge, 1996).

9. See also Michael Marmot, "Contribution of Psychosocial Factors to Socioeconomic Differences in Health," *Milibank Quarterly* 76 (1998): pp. 403–408.

NORMAN DANIELS, BRUCE KENNEDY, AND
ICHIRO KAWACHI / *Justice Is Good for Our Health*

1. John Rawls, *A Theory of Justice*, rev. ed. (Cambridge: Harvard University Press, Belknap Press, 1999).

2. See Richard G. Wilkinson, *Unhealthy Societies: The Afflictions of Inequality* (London: Routledge, 1996).

3. John W. Lynch et al., "Income Inequality and Mortality in Metropolitan Areas of the United States," *American Journal of Public Health* 88 (1998): 1074–1080.

4. Ichiro Kawachi, Bruce Kennedy, and Richard G. Wilkinson, *Income Inequality and Health: A Reader* (New York: New Press, 1999).

5. See Douglas Black et al., *Inequalities in Health: The Black Report, the Health Divide* (London: Penguin Group, 1988).

6. Michael Marmot et al., "Contribution of Psychosocial Factors to Socioeconomic Differences in Health," *Milbank Quarterly* 76 (1998): 403–408.

7. Bruce Kennedy et al., "Income Distribution, Socioeconomic Status, and Self-Rated Health: A U.S. Multi-Level Analysis," *British Medical Journal* 317 (1998): 917–921.

8. For example, the correlation between social capital, as measured by low interpersonal trust, and the maximum welfare grant, as a percent of state per capita income, is −.76. See Kawachi et al., "Social Capital, Income Inequality, and Mortality," *American Journal of Public Health* 87 (1997): 1491–1498.

9. Goran Dahlgren and Margaret Whitehead, *Policies and Strategies to Promote Social Equality in Health* (Stockholm: Institute of Future Studies, 1991).

10. This essay is a revised and substantially edited version of an article published in *Daedalus*, "Why Justice Is Good for Our Health: The Social Determinants of Health Inequalities," *Daedalus*, vol. 128, no. 2 (Fall

1999): 215–51. Norman Daniels, Bruce Kennedy, and Ichiro Kawachi wrote this essay during their tenure as Robert Wood Johnson Investigator Awardees.

TED MARMOR / *Policy Options*

1. Harold Pollack, delivered at the October 1999 meetings of the American Association of Programs in Policy Analysis and Management, in Washington, D.C.

EMMANUELA GAKIDOU, JULIO FRENK, AND CHRISTOPHER MURRAY / *A Health Agenda*

1. The cost of being fully informed about the health consequences of different choices often is prohibitively high. Most individuals are forced to make choices with incomplete or incorrect information. When the choice to take on risk and the outcome are separated in time, the rate at which individuals discount the future can profoundly influence choices about health.

ABOUT THE CONTRIBUTORS

SUDHIR ANAND is professor of economics at Oxford University and adjunct professor at the Harvard School of Public Health.

MARCIA ANGELL is a physician and editor-in-chief of the *New England Journal of Medicine*.

JOSHUA COHEN is professor of philosophy and Sloan Professor of Political Science at the Massachusetts Institute of Technology. He is editor-in-chief of *Boston Review* and author of numerous books and articles in political theory.

NORMAN DANIELS is Goldthwaite Professor of Philosophy at Tufts. He is author of *Justice and Justification: Reflective Equilibrium in Theory and Practice*.

EZEKIEL EMANUEL is chair of the department of clinical bioethics at the Warren G. Magnuson Clinical Center of the National Institutes of Health and a breast oncologist.

EMMANUELA GAKIDOU, JULIO FRENK, and CHRISTOPHER MURRAY work for the World Health Organization's global program on evidence for health policy.

ICHIRO KAWACHI is director of the Harvard Center for Society and Health. He is coeditor of the *Reader on Income Inequality and Health*.

BRUCE KENNEDY is assistant professor of health and social behavior at the Harvard School of Public Health.

TED MARMOR is professor of public policy at Yale and author of *The Politics of Medicare*.

MICHAEL MARMOT is professor of epidemiology and public health at University College London, and director, International Centre for Health and Society.

ABOUT THE CONTRIBUTORS

FABIENNE PETER is assistant professor of economics at the University of Basel.

JOEL ROGERS is professor of law, political science, and sociology at the University of Wisconsin, a member of the *Boston Review* editorial board, and author of numerous articles and books on American politics.

AMARTYA SEN received the Nobel Prize in Economics in 1998. He teaches at Trinity College, Cambridge University.

BARBARA STARFIELD is University Distinguished Professor at The Johns Hopkins Medical Institutions.

STEFFIE WOOLHANDLER and DAVID HIMMELSTEIN practice and teach internal medicine in Cambridge, Massachusetts. They are vocal proponents of national health insurance.